NASA'S JUNO SPACECRAFT LAUNCHES ON AN ATLAS V ROCKET FROM CAPE CANAVERAL, FLORIDA, U.S.A., IN AUGUST 2011. JUNO'S MISSION WAS TO STUDY JUPITER AND ITS ATMOSPHERE AND MAGNETIC FIELD, AMONG OTHER INVESTIGATIONS OF THE PLANET.

THE SUN RISES ON THE INTERNATIONAL SPACE STATION IN 2009. THE PHOTO WAS TAKEN BY A CREW MEMBER ABOARD THE STATION.

NATIONAL GEOGRAPHIC
KiDS

Absolute Expert
SPACE

All the
LATEST
FACTS From
the Field

Joan Marie Galat

With National Geographic Explorer
Munazza Alam

NATIONAL GEOGRAPHIC
Washington, D.C.

CONTENTS

FOREWORD by National Geographic
Explorer Munazza Alam 6

CHAPTER 1
What's Up? 8

EXPLORER INTRODUCTION 10
Where Does Space Begin? 12
Distances in Space 13
Everything Is Moving: Gravity's
    Influence 14
Motion in Space 16
What's Goin' Round? 17
Our Place in Space 18
Over the Moon: What's Out There? 20
Elements 23
Sun Huggers and Gas Giants 24
Dwarf Planets and Beyond 36
Comets and Meteoroids 40
SPACE WATCH: Spot a Meteor! 42
SPACE LAB: Gravity Games 44

CHAPTER 2
Beyond Our Solar System 46

EXPLORER INTRODUCTION 48
Stars Under Construction 50
Main Sequence Stars 50
Giant Stars 51
Dwarf Stars 52
When a Star Collapses 53
Invisible Stars 54
Bright Today, Dim Tomorrow 55
On the Bright Side 56
Seeing Double 57
Hot Jupiters 58
Brighter Than a Trillion Suns 60
Light From Gas 60
Neutron Stars 63
SPACE WATCH: Spot These Bright
    Stars! 64
SPACE LAB: Make a Model of a
    Black Hole 66

CHAPTER 4

Our Universe 92

EXPLORER INTRODUCTION............. 94
The Big Bang.. 96
Clusters of Galaxies.......................... 96
Dark Matter and Dark Energy 97
Hello Out There................................... 98
Are We Alone?..................................... 98
Lights Out!...100
Space Jobs 101
Three Ways to See the Night Sky 103
SPACE WATCH: Spot a Naked-Eye
    Galaxy!..104
SPACE LAB: Bend Light—Reflection
    and Refraction in Action 106

GLOSSARY 108
INDEX 109
CREDITS 111

CHAPTER 3

Journey to Space 68

EXPLORER INTRODUCTION............. 70
Why Explore Space?.......................... 72
Exploring From Earth........................ 72
Exploring From Space 74
The International Space Station 81
Early Space Stations........................ 82
Space Litter 83
Ready, Set, Go—to Space!................. 84
Space Technology Spin-Offs 85
Donning a Suit for Space................... 85
A Day on the ISS................................. 86
How Can You Become an Astronaut? .. 87
SPACE WATCH: Spot a Satellite or
    Space Junk! 88
SPACE LAB: Make a Rocket! 90

MUNAZZA ALAM

MUNAZZA STUDIES HOT JUPITERS, WHICH ARE HUGE EXOPLANETS, OR PLANETS OUTSIDE OF OUR SOLAR SYSTEM.

FOREWORD

Hi, my name is Munazza Alam. I'm an astronomer. I love astronomy because I love looking up at the night sky. Seeing some of the 300 billion stars in the Milky Way galaxy, I can't help but wonder what else is out there. This curiosity about the universe and our place in it is not new. For thousands of years, humans all over the world have gazed up at the sky and wondered, "Are we alone?"

I try to answer this question by studying exoplanets, or planets outside of the solar system. I want to know what these planets are like. Are they similar to Earth? Are they similar to other planets in our solar system? One way to understand these planets is by studying their atmospheres. Exoplanet atmospheres can tell us about the climate of these planets, as well as how they formed and evolved over time.

I learn about exoplanet atmospheres by using data from the Hubble Space Telescope. I observe these planets when they transit, or pass in front of, their host stars (the stars they orbit around). When a planet is passing in front of its star, we know that the planet is there, but we can't actually see it. That's because the star is so much brighter than the planet. It's like looking at a firefly close to a lamp. You can see a firefly glow on a dark night, but it's really hard to see one next to a bright lightbulb! Similarly, when a planet is in front of its star during transit, we can't see it—but we will see a dip in the brightness of the star. That's because the planet

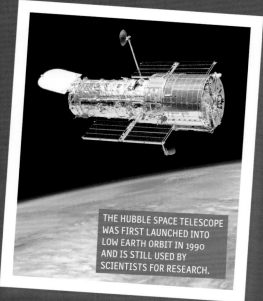

THE HUBBLE SPACE TELESCOPE WAS FIRST LAUNCHED INTO LOW EARTH ORBIT IN 1990 AND IS STILL USED BY SCIENTISTS FOR RESEARCH.

blocks out some of the star's light during transit. The size of that dip is proportional to the size of the planet.

We can measure this dip in different wavelengths, or colors, of light. If the planet has an atmosphere, the size of the dip will be bigger or smaller at different wavelengths, depending on what the planet's atmosphere is made up of. When a planet transits its star, we measure the size of the dip by observing different colors of light. These colors also tell us what the atmosphere is like. This technique has helped us detect clouds and hazes on exoplanets that are millions of miles away—but there is still so much left to discover!

Look for me throughout the book as we explore the universe!

—Munazza Alam

THE AURORA BOREALIS LIGHTS UP THE WINTER SKY IN THE LOFOTEN ISLANDS, NORWAY.

CHAPTER 1

WHAT'S UP?

HOW DID I BECOME AN ASTRONOMER?

I grew up in New York City, famously known as "the city that never sleeps." In New York, the city lights outshine the stars at night. Growing up, I was accustomed to a view of the sky in which I could only see a handful of stars at a time—at best!

MUNAZZA ALAM

I found my love for astronomy in college. I went to Hunter College in New York City, where I studied physics. Physics is the study of matter and energy, and how they interact. I wanted to study physics in college because I was always curious to learn how things work and I enjoy problem-solving.

As a college student, I worked in the Astrophysics Department at the American Museum of Natural History. To collect data for my work, I have visited observatories in exciting places like Arizona and Hawaii in the United States, and Chile. The observatories I have visited are home to powerful telescopes that can be used to observe faraway, faint objects. Some of these telescopes are the size of a school bus!

Telescopes work by collecting particles of light called photons. We can think of them as "light buckets"—the bigger the telescope, the more light it can collect.

But in order to understand the light collected, we mount instruments on telescopes that can split the light into its colors.

My first observing experience was at the Kitt Peak National Observatory, just outside Tucson, Arizona. There, I got my first glimpse of what it meant and what it felt like to be an astronomer. I was instantly hooked! It was the first time I had ever been to a desert, the first time I had ever been on a mountain, and the first time I had ever truly seen a dark night sky.

It was a breathtaking sight to see hundreds of thousands of stars. Seeing the Milky Way for the first time reminded me how vast and mysterious the universe is—and I wanted to help unlock some of its secrets.

HALLEY'S COMET

HALLEY'S COMET IS ONE OF THE OBJECTS IN SPACE THAT WE CAN SEE WITH THE NAKED EYE. HERE IT IS OVER THE SUPERSTITION MOUNTAINS IN ARIZONA, U.S.A., ON ITS LAST VISIT IN 1986.

TO OBSERVE OBJECTS IN SPACE, ASTRONOMERS USE MASSIVE TELESCOPES HOUSED IN OBSERVATORIES.

KITT PEAK NATIONAL OBSERVATORY IN ARIZONA, U.S.A., HOUSES THREE MAJOR NIGHTTIME TELESCOPES, PLUS TWO RADIO TELESCOPES AND 22 OPTICAL TELESCOPES.

THE UNIVERSE HOLDS EVERYTHING THAT EXISTS.

It includes stars, planets, galaxies, every form of matter—even matter that we can't see—time, and energy.

Where Does Space Begin?

You look up on a clear night and gaze skyward. Faraway stars in the endless black sky show you the universe is vast. Something speeds across the sky, blinking. It's a satellite, reminding you that people are using machines and technology to explore space. So much lies beyond Planet Earth. A dark, remote location lets you see stars, planets, and the spiraling arm of our Milky Way galaxy. The galaxy contains billions of stars, as well as objects you can see without a telescope, including meteors, star clusters, and fuzzy clouds of gas and dust. How can you not wonder about what else is up there? Where does space begin, and how far can you see?

Most scientists agree that space begins where Earth's atmosphere ends, but where might that be? Earth's atmosphere is made up of different layers of gases—mostly nitrogen and oxygen, plus smaller amounts of other gases—that surround the planet. This blanket of air makes life possible, trapping oxygen to breathe and heat to keep us warm. There is no clear line between the atmosphere and space because the last layer does not just suddenly stop. Instead, the atmosphere becomes less dense as it extends upward. Things begin to change 62 miles (100 km) above Earth. At this height, the atmosphere no longer holds enough air to support an airplane in flight. This boundary, measured from sea level, is the edge of space. It's called the Kármán Line, after Theodore Van Kármán, a Hungarian-American aerospace engineer who lived from 1881 to 1963. He calculated that objects above and below this altitude travel differently because of the amount of air present. Airplanes need air to stay aloft, so they must fly below the Kármán Line. Above the Kármán Line, it takes a rocket to fly higher.

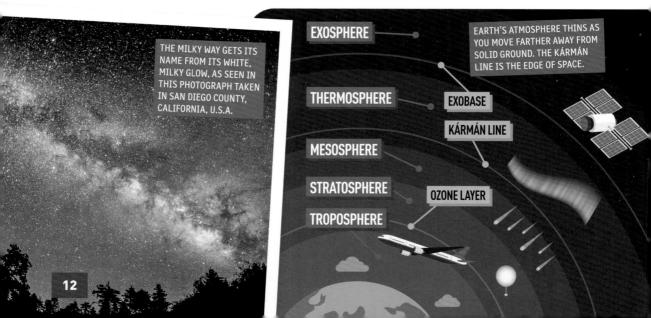

THE MILKY WAY GETS ITS NAME FROM ITS WHITE, MILKY GLOW, AS SEEN IN THIS PHOTOGRAPH TAKEN IN SAN DIEGO COUNTY, CALIFORNIA, U.S.A.

EXOSPHERE

EARTH'S ATMOSPHERE THINS AS YOU MOVE FARTHER AWAY FROM SOLID GROUND. THE KÁRMÁN LINE IS THE EDGE OF SPACE.

THERMOSPHERE

EXOBASE

KÁRMÁN LINE

MESOSPHERE

STRATOSPHERE

OZONE LAYER

TROPOSPHERE

Beyond the Kármán Line, a new world begins: space. It contains the moon, the sun, and all the planets and moons in our solar system. Space is home to star systems with their own planets and moons, as well as comets, meteors, and asteroids. It contains gases, dust particles, and galaxies rich with celestial objects. Our vast universe includes black holes, quasars, pulsars, dark matter, and dark energy. You can even find human-made objects beyond Earth! Scientists have sent robots and spacecraft into space, including rovers to Mars and a probe to explore Pluto (see Exploring From Space, page 74). From high above, satellites, telescopes, and space stations circle Earth. And most exciting of all, since November 2000, people have been continually living in space! That's right—astronauts on missions can live on the International Space Station for about six months at a time. More on that later! (See page 81.)

AURORAS GLOW A GHOSTLY GREEN OVER THE FJORDS OF NORWAY.

Distances in Space

Day or night, you look into space every time you look into the sky. The nearest space phenomena you can see at night are the northern and southern lights. Called auroras, the lights ripple overhead at heights from 60 to 620 miles (97 to 1,000 km) above Earth. The moon is the closest object—but it's not that close. Imagine 30 Earths between us and the moon. Its average distance from Earth is 238,855 miles (384,400 km) away. Venus is the closest planet, averaging a distance of about 25 million miles (40 million km) away from Earth.

You feel the effects of the closest star to Earth every single day. That star is our sun, at 93 million miles (150 million km) away. During the day, light and heat energy from the sun travel through outer space and reach Earth, giving you light to see and heat to warm your skin. The sun's light is not like switching on a lamp, though. It takes a little more than eight minutes for sunlight to reach Earth.

LOTS OF EMPTY SPACE

WHILE SPACE IS THE REGION BEYOND EARTH'S ATMOSPHERE, "space" is also a word that refers to "having room." In outer space, there is lots of room! Most of space is empty. It is a vacuum—a cold, empty space where nothing exists. On Earth, the atmosphere scatters light, making the sky blue in the day and a bit orange or pink at sunrise and sunset. In space, there is no air to bend light. The sky is always black. Sound waves need air to travel through, so the lack of air makes it quiet, too. If you could sing "Twinkle, Twinkle, Little Star" in space, no one would hear you, even if you sang at the top of your voice.

THE SKY IS ALWAYS BLACK IN SPACE. IN THIS PHOTO, TAKEN BY A CREW MEMBER ON THE INTERNATIONAL SPACE STATION, AN ORBITAL SUNRISE REFLECTS OFF THE ROUND CURVE OF EARTH.

Beyond the sun, it's hard to describe distances in miles. The numbers get too big. Scientists solved this problem by describing distances in space in light-years. A light-year is the distance light can travel in one year. It equals 5.88 trillion miles (9.46 trillion km). That means when you are looking at a star 200 light-years away, you are seeing the light that left that star 200 years ago.

Beyond our sun, the nearest stars belong to the Alpha Centauri star system. The three stars that make up this group are an average of 4.3 light-years from Earth. Even though these distances are great, you can see these stars shining in the night sky—and you can see objects even farther away, too. The farthest object the naked eye can see is the Andromeda galaxy (M31), 2.5 million light-years away. That means your eyes can look back in time 2.5 million years. Astronomers using telescopes can look back into the universe 13.8 billion light-years—in every direction. Why stop there? The universe is thought to be about 13.8 billion years old.

ALPHA CENTAURI A (LEFT) AND B (RIGHT) MAKE UP THE NEAREST STAR SYSTEM TO EARTH.

Everything Is Moving: Gravity's Influence

You are on Earth right now because of gravity. It's the invisible force that stops you from floating skyward. It is also the reason you can live on Earth. Gravity is like an invisible glue that keeps the atmosphere anchored to the planet. Without it, even the oxygen you need to breathe would float away!

Gravity works the same in every part of the universe. Every object exerts a gravitational force—pulling objects toward its center. Gravity is the chief force that affects how objects move in space. It can cause objects to move in different directions or even crash together.

The strength of gravity depends on two things. One is distance. When objects are close to one another, gravity is strongest. When objects are far apart, gravity is weaker. Gravity's strength also depends on mass—the actual amount of

INVISIBLE FORCES

GRAVITY CAUSES ALL OBJECTS to move at the same speed, whether they are large or small. On Earth, however, air creates resistance, called drag, which can make one object slower than another. You can *feel* the impact of air resistance when you ride your bike fast. When you lean forward, the air resistance lessens. You can *see* how air affects gravity by dropping a feather and tennis ball at the same time. In a vacuum, they would both land at the same time. On Earth, air slows the feather.

YOU CAN FEEL THE INVISIBLE FORCE OF DRAG WHEN RIDING A BIKE.

WEIGH OUT THERE!

MASS MEASURES THE AMOUNT OF MATERIAL an object contains. Weight measures gravitational force by describing how light or heavy an object is at a particular location. This chart lists what the same items would weigh on the moon, Mars, Earth, and Jupiter.

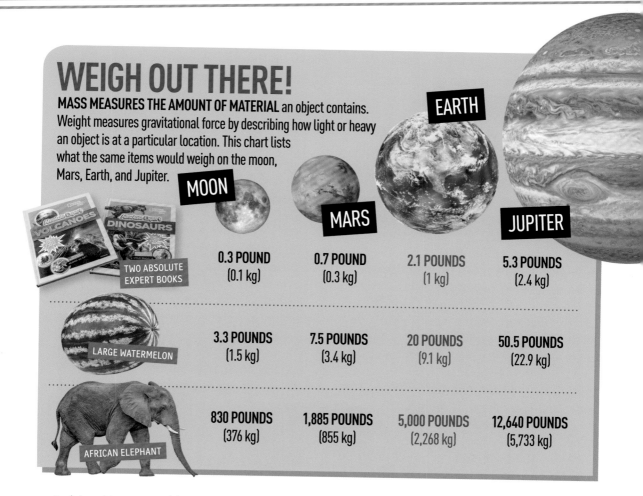

	MOON	MARS	EARTH	JUPITER
TWO ABSOLUTE EXPERT BOOKS	0.3 POUND (0.1 kg)	0.7 POUND (0.3 kg)	2.1 POUNDS (1 kg)	5.3 POUNDS (2.4 kg)
LARGE WATERMELON	3.3 POUNDS (1.5 kg)	7.5 POUNDS (3.4 kg)	20 POUNDS (9.1 kg)	50.5 POUNDS (22.9 kg)
AFRICAN ELEPHANT	830 POUNDS (376 kg)	1,885 POUNDS (855 kg)	5,000 POUNDS (2,268 kg)	12,640 POUNDS (5,733 kg)

material making up an object. Massive celestial objects, like the sun, have more gravity than smaller objects, like the moon. Gravity causes the high and low tides of Earth's oceans. The tides are mostly caused by gravity from the moon. But the gravity of our massive sun also plays a role, even though it is much farther away.

The sun's strong gravity causes the planets to travel around it in orbit—a regular path that one object follows around another. It's like a tetherball spinning around a pole. Think of the top of the pole as the sun, the ball as Earth, and the string as the pull of gravity. Sideways motion keeps the ball orbiting the pole. On Earth, air resistance, or friction from the rope, slows the ball as it travels around the pole. Eventually, the ball hits the pole and stops orbiting. The planets don't get pulled into the sun, though. They are moving too fast! In the case of the planets, this friction does not exist, so the planets keep orbiting, never reaching the sun.

The force of gravity is measured by describing how much something weighs. While mass never changes, weight can change. Weight depends on gravity's strength at a location in space. If you could stand on Earth's moon, your mass would be the same as it is on Earth, but your weight would be lower due to the moon's weaker gravity. If you weigh 100 pounds (45 kg) on Earth, you would weigh 17 pounds (8 kg) on the moon.

Motion in Space

Everything in space is moving, including you! Just as Earth spins on its axis, all objects in space rotate. Earth completes one spin every 24 hours, which makes one Earth day. Earth's rotation, measured at the Equator, is about 1,000 miles an hour (1,600 km/h). Even though that's awfully fast, you can't feel it because you're traveling through space at the same speed.

Planets, stars, and most other space objects also travel in an orbit. Moons orbit planets, and planets orbit stars. The planets in our solar system orbit the sun as it follows its own path around the center of the Milky Way. Every 230 million years, our solar system completes an orbit around the center of the Milky Way.

Scientists estimate that the Milky Way has more than 250 billion stars. (It's difficult to count stars! Astronomers must examine a sample section of the galaxy, then make an estimate.) These stars are moving, too. They revolve around the center of the Milky Way, like a massive whirlpool. Some galaxies belong to groups of galaxies called clusters. Clusters also move, orbiting the group's center. At the same time, all galaxies are also moving away from each other as the universe expands (see The Big Bang, page 96). Space objects really get around!

How Objects Move in Space

Sir Isaac Newton (1643–1727), a physicist and mathematician from England, figured out three laws of motion. He explained, for the first time, how objects move in space.

Newton's first law says an object at rest will not start moving by itself, and an object will travel in a straight line, at the same speed, until a force makes it stop or change direction. This is a fancy way of saying that an object will keep doing what it's doing unless something makes it change. An object that resists change in motion experiences a property called inertia. You can feel it when you're in a car that swings hard around a corner. Your body wants to keep going in the same direction—straight—and you feel a pull. In space, a spacecraft far from any source of gravity will continue in one direction, at a constant speed, until a force—like the blast of a rocket—makes it stop or change direction.

Newton's second law says the harder you push an object, the farther and faster it will move. Imagine you're a batter in a softball game. You bunt the first pitch and the ball falls short. Next time, you swing hard and the ball flies far. It just might be a home run, but if the ball bounces off an outfielder's glove, the impact will send it in a different direction. Now imagine what would happen if you could hit a ball into space, far away from any source of gravity. After it finished accelerating, the ball would travel at a constant speed. It would only stop if it hit another object or encountered another force.

Newton's third law states that when you push an object, it will push back in the opposite direction with the same amount of force. Suppose you lie on the ground and push it. What happens? As you push on Earth, it pushes back. Since Earth is more massive than you are, you move, and the result is a push-up. Forces always come in pairs: There's an action and a reaction. If an astronaut floating in a spacecraft threw an object, the astronaut would move in the opposite direction.

SOFTBALL HELPS DEMONSTRATE NEWTON'S SECOND LAW OF MOTION.

WHAT'S GOIN' ROUND?

OBJECTS IN ORBIT ARE CALLED SATELLITES. There are natural satellites, such as moons, that orbit the planets. There are also artificial satellites. These are machines that humans have placed in space to collect and transmit information. Artificial satellites orbit Earth and can be placed in orbit around other planets, too.

Rather than following perfect circles, all orbit paths are ellipses—slightly flattened circles, or ovals. Planet orbits are almost circular, but comet orbits are more egg-shaped. The more squashed an object's orbit, the less circular its path, which is called eccentric. Most objects, in most solar systems, lie in an orbital plane. This flat, plate-like area passes through the center of an object, like our sun, and extends to the edge of its solar system. The planets do not run into each other because they lie in or near the same plane. Some comets, however, travel outside the orbital plane, or at an angle to it. This is one of the reasons why comets, on rare occasions, can strike planets.

NEPTUNE: 3.4 miles/s (5.4 km/s)

JUPITER: 8.1 miles/s (13 km/s)

URANUS: 4.2 miles/s (6.8 km/s)

SATURN: 6 miles/s (9.7 km/s)

MARS: 15 miles/s (24.1 km/s)

EARTH: 18.5 miles/s (29.8 km/s)

MERCURY: 29.4 miles/s (47.3 km/s)

VENUS: 21.8 miles/s (35 km/s)

ORBITAL VELOCITY IS THE AVERAGE SPEED OF A PLANET as it loops around the sun.

Our Place in Space

Rich with mystery, our vast universe reaches far beyond what we can see. Starting at Earth and exploring outward reveals amazing facts about our place in space. Every year, astronomers make exciting new discoveries. But each one raises fresh questions.

Planet Earth

Planet Earth is a special place. It has an atmosphere, liquid water, and the only known life in the universe. Earth is a terrestrial planet, or a rocky planet with a hard surface. Similar to other terrestrial planets, Earth has a crust, mantle, and core, and landscapes that include mountains, valleys, volcanoes, and craters. Mercury, Venus, and Mars are terrestrial planets, too, but Earth is the largest. Water covers about 71 percent of our planet.

Solar System

Earth is part of a gigantic neighborhood called the solar system, a group of objects in space that orbit the sun. Our neighborhood includes eight planets and their moons, as well as dwarf planets, asteroids, comets, and meteoroids. Small rocky objects, called asteroids, are also found in the solar system. So far, 795,076 asteroids have been counted. Most asteroids orbit the sun in the asteroid belt, which lies between the planets Mars and Jupiter. The solar system is also home to dwarf planets Pluto, Ceres, Eris, Haumea, and Makemake. Ceres is located in the asteroid belt, while Pluto, Eris, Haumea, and Makemake lie beyond Neptune in the Kuiper belt, a massive region where comets and other celestial bodies are found. ("Kuiper" rhymes with "piper.") Our solar system stretches about nine billion miles (15 billion km) from the sun and hurtles through the Milky Way at 515,000 miles an hour (828,800 km/h).

Scientists believe the solar system formed 4.6 billion years ago from a giant cloud of dust and gas. The dense cloud collapsed into a flat, spinning disk called a solar nebula. A shock wave from a nearby star, exploding into a supernova, may have triggered the collapse. Over time, gravity caused the dust and gas to collect at the disk's center. A reaction called nuclear fusion would have taken place.

EARTH IS UNIQUE IN OUR SOLAR SYSTEM BECAUSE IT HAS LIQUID WATER AND THE ONLY KNOWN LIFE-FORMS.

OUR GALACTIC ADDRESS: EARTH, SOLAR SYSTEM, MILKY WAY GALAXY (PICTURED HERE), LOCAL GROUP, LOCAL SUPERCLUSTER, LANIAKEA SUPERCLUSTER, UNIVERSE

As hydrogen fused into helium, the sun formed, using up 99 percent of the dust and gas. As gravity brought clumps of the remaining dust and gas together, planets, moons, asteroids, and comets were created. Astronomers also believe the entire solar system is surrounded by a region called the Oort cloud, which may contain more than a trillion icy objects.

The Milky Way

The Milky Way looks like a pathway of light in our night sky, but that is just part of the picture. It is really a disk, with arms that spiral outward. Its stars are spread across a region so vast, it takes 100,000 years for light to cross it. Our solar system is located on the inner edge of an area called the Orion Arm, about halfway from the galaxy's center.

Clusters and Superclusters

Most galaxies are part of a cluster of galaxies, brought together by gravity. The Milky Way belongs to a cluster of about 50 galaxies called the Local Group. The galaxies of the Local Group are spread across an area that spans a diameter of 10 million light-years. Clusters are the largest structures in the universe because gravity binds them together. Yet even larger groups have been discovered.

Superclusters are collections of galaxy clusters. The Local Group is part of the local supercluster, also called the Virgo supercluster. It's located near an outer edge, while the enormous 2,000-galaxy Virgo cluster lies at the center of the local (Virgo) supercluster. Our local supercluster is in an even larger group called Laniakea, which includes more than 100,000 galaxies. *Laniakea* is a Hawaiian word meaning "immeasurable heaven."

The Universe

The universe is everything on Earth, everything in space, and all the empty space. It includes all matter and all types of energy, and it even includes time. No one knows how big the universe is because it is continually expanding at a very high speed. We can't see its edge, and scientists aren't sure it has one. We do know that the part of the universe we can now see is 93 billion light-years across. This is called the observable universe.

FARAWAY GALAXY CLUSTERS SWIRL LIGHT-YEARS AWAY FROM EARTH. THESE CLUSTERS ARE IN THE DIRECTION OF CONSTELLATIONS CENTAURUS AND HYDRA.

WE ARE HERE

SOLAR FLARE

THIS IMAGE OF THE SUN WAS CAPTURED USING AN EXTREME ULTRAVIOLET IMAGING TELESCOPE.

Over the Moon: What's Out There?

Nuclear reactions deep inside the sun are the source of all its energy. After taking up to a million years to travel from the sun's core to its surface, the sun's energy reaches Earth in minutes. Light and heat from the sun make life on Earth possible.

What Makes Our Sun?

You've felt the sun's warm energy your entire life, but what exactly is that yellow ball in the sky? Is it a solid, liquid, or gas? In fact, the sun is made of plasma! Some call plasma the fourth state of matter. The most common forms of matter on Earth are solids, liquids, and gases, but plasma—an electrically charged gas—is the most common type of matter found in the universe. While a regular gas has no electrical charge, plasma contains both positively and negatively charged particles that can form magnetic currents and electric fields. Plasma forms during nuclear fusion—a process that happens in the sun's core—and is the reason the sun shines.

Nuclear fusion happens when the nuclei of two atoms join together. It takes place in the sun's core when gravity, which holds the sun's mass together, compresses gas. This creates great pressure and very high temperatures. Here's how nuclear fusion occurs in the sun: Pressure in the core fuses four hydrogen nuclei together. These fused hydrogen nuclei create a larger helium nucleus. The process releases vast amounts of energy in the form of heat and light. Inside the sun, more than 600 million tons (544,000,000 t) of hydrogen are turned into helium every second. This creates a flow of hot plasma, called the solar wind. Although you can't feel or see the solar wind, it travels out from the sun in every direction. The solar wind forms the sun's magnetic field, which stretches through the solar system.

The sun is very active. Shifting magnetic fields form sunspots, which appear as dark spots on the sun's surface. Explosions of energy, called solar flares, appear as flashes of light that can last from minutes to hours. More powerful explosions cause coronal mass ejections (CMEs) that send plasma toward Earth at a million miles an hour. The sun also produces ultraviolet rays, x-rays, and other kinds of radiation. If you've ever had a suntan or sunburn, you know what radiation from the sun can do!

Like Earth, the sun rotates on its axis, but it does not rotate at one speed, because it's not a solid object like Earth. The sun's equator and poles each rotate at much different speeds because the sun is made of plasma. One day, or full rotation, at the sun's equator equals about 25 Earth days, but one day at the sun's poles lasts about 36 Earth days.

Whoa, That's Big!

The sun's shape is a nearly perfect sphere, and it is large enough to hold 1.3 million Earths! Closer to us than all the other stars, it appears big in our sky, but as you will see a little later, much larger stars exist. The sun is actually a medium-size star, called a yellow dwarf. Yellow dwarfs are main sequence stars, which means they fuse hydrogen into

ALL THE PLANETS IN OUR SOLAR SYSTEM COULD FIT INSIDE THE SUN—WITH PLENTY OF ROOM TO SPARE!

THE VIEW OF THE SUN FROM EARTH AS IT RISES OVER THE SAVANNA IN KENYA, AFRICA.

SUN STATS

RADIUS	432,168.6 miles (695,508 km)
ORBIT SPEED AROUND THE GALAXY	450,000 miles an hour (724,200 km/h)
SPIN RATE AT EQUATOR	Once about every 25 days
SPIN RATE AT POLES	Once every 36 days
TIME TO ORBIT THE MILKY WAY	230 million years
TEMPERATURE AT CORE	27 million degrees Fahrenheit (15 million degrees Celsius)
TEMPERATURE AT SURFACE	10,000 degrees Fahrenheit (5,540 degrees Celsius)

helium in their cores. Yellow dwarfs have a surface temperature around 9711°F (5377°C) and exist for about 10 billion years.

While you know the sun is the center of our solar system, you might be surprised to discover its mass equals 99.8 percent of the mass of everything in the solar system. That means most of the solar system is the sun. The planets and their moons, along with every asteroid, comet, atom of gas, and particle of dust, including you, make up the other 0.2 percent.

The Changing Sun

Like all stars, the sun has a life cycle. It was born, it will exist for a period of time, and it will eventually die. The sun is 4.5 billion years old, but it's only about halfway through its life. Astronomers are able to estimate its age by looking at how long its hydrogen will take to

LAYERS OF THE SUN

THE SUN IS MADE UP OF DIFFERENT LAYERS.
The **CORE**, at the center, produces the sun's energy, which travels upward through the **RADIATIVE ZONE**, a trip that takes about 170,000 years. The light particles continue to the next layer—the **CONVECTION ZONE**—but now energy travels more quickly, like bubbling gases pushing outward. The sun's next layers make up its atmosphere. The **PHOTOSPHERE** is the sun's surface, and its light is visible to the human eye. This region, 300 miles (480 km) thick, is where sunspots appear. The **CHROMOSPHERE** is a thin layer of plasma, with temperatures up to tens of thousands of degrees. When viewed during an eclipse, the chromosphere glows red, while the plumes of the outermost layer, the **CORONA**, appear white.

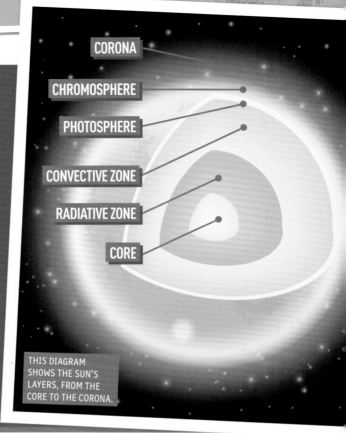

CORONA

CHROMOSPHERE

PHOTOSPHERE

CONVECTIVE ZONE

RADIATIVE ZONE

CORE

THIS DIAGRAM SHOWS THE SUN'S LAYERS, FROM THE CORE TO THE CORONA.

fuse into helium. The sun will burn for about another five billion years, and then it will start to change. When its core runs out of hydrogen, the nuclear reaction in the core will stop. The core will collapse and grow hotter. Hydrogen outside the core will fuse, and heat inside the core will push the sun's outer layers outward. The sun will grow larger and cooler as it becomes a different kind of star, called a red giant. As the red giant expands, its heat will dry up the water on Earth, and life will no longer exist. The sun will grow 2,000 times brighter, continuing as a red giant for a period

A RED GIANT EXPANDS AS IT COOLS, TURNING RED.

that may last from a few thousand to a billion years. Eventually, it will become a smaller kind of star called a white dwarf, which is a dead star made up of oxygen and carbon. The white dwarf forms after all the red giant's outer layers are ejected, leaving only the core. As a white dwarf, the sun will contain its original mass but be closer to the size of Earth. Like a fire that's run out of fuel, it will emit light and heat for a period. After about 10 billion years, the glow will disappear, and a black dwarf will remain. No black dwarfs exist, because the universe is too young for one to have formed yet.

ELEMENTS

ELEMENTS ARE ALL AROUND YOU! An element is the simplest form of a pure substance. Each one contains only one kind of atom (see The Big Bang, page 96). When combined with other kinds of elements, they make up all the matter in the world. Pure elements include substances like hydrogen, helium, sodium, calcium, copper, iron, and gold. Elements combined with other elements are called compounds. You might be surprised by how many you know. Two hydrogen atoms and one oxygen atom make water; one carbon atom and two oxygen atoms make carbon dioxide; and one sodium atom and one chlorine atom make table salt.

Elements are listed in the Periodic Table of Elements. Each element has an abbreviation and an atomic number, which indicates how many protons exist in a single atom. (Protons are small, positively charged particles in the nucleus of an atom.) Elements are separated into groups, including metals, nonmetals, and metalloids—elements like silicon and arsenic, which have characteristics of both other types. Metals are shiny elements that conduct electricity and are sometimes magnetic. They are also malleable—able to be shaped and bent without breaking. Aluminum, nickel, and zinc are metals. Nonmetals are elements that are dull, nonmagnetic, and not usually able to conduct electricity. Oxygen, helium, and carbon are nonmetals.

Most natural elements formed in outer space. Light elements like hydrogen and helium came from the big bang. Nuclear fusion in stars creates elements, too, like carbon and oxygen, while supernovae create all the elements heavier than iron, including copper, mercury, gold, and lead.

SOME METALS ARE MAGNETIC, LIKE THIS TOY.

THE ELEMENT HELIUM HELPS THIS BLIMP TO FLOAT.

THE MOST COMMON ELEMENT

MOST OF THE SOLAR SYSTEM is made up of hydrogen—an element with no color, smell, or taste. In fact, most of the universe is made up of hydrogen. Along with oxygen, hydrogen is in every drop of water. It is in Earth's crust and atmosphere and in every plant and animal. The sun contains about 70.6 percent hydrogen and 27.4 percent helium. Together, carbon, nitrogen, and oxygen make up around 1.5 percent. The rest includes small amounts of neon, iron, silicon, magnesium, and sulfur.

ASTEROID BELT

Sun Huggers and Gas Giants

While stars create their own light, all planets reflect light. If you could strap on a jet pack and explore our solar system, you would find two different types of planets. The terrestrial planets, closest to the sun, are the inner planets. The gas giants, on the other side of the asteroid belt, are outer planets. The inner planets—Mercury, Venus, Earth, and Mars—are small compared to the gas giants. They may have one or two moons, or no moon at all. These sun huggers have other things in common, too. They're rocky, dense, and rounder than the outer planets. Their solid surfaces are the reason the inner planets are called the terrestrial planets. *Terra* is the Latin word for land.

The inner planets have thin atmospheres around large rocky bodies, while the outer planets—Jupiter, Saturn, Uranus, and Neptune— have thick atmospheres around small dense cores. Also called the Jovian planets, the outer planets are a bit thick in the middle, making their shapes slightly oblong. They can have dozens of moons, and each planet has rings, with Saturn's being the most famous. Surrounded by gases, the outer planets have no solid surface, making it impossible to land on one. If you could travel through the gas, you would reach liquid hydrogen and helium. Better not stop!

ITALIAN ASTRONOMER GALILEO GALILEI MADE NEW DISCOVERIES BY PEERING INTO THE NIGHT SKY WITH A SPYGLASS.

Moons and the Big Splash

We call the white orb circling our planet "the moon" because we knew about it first. All other natural satellites orbiting planets and asteroids are simply called moons. So far, more than 190 moons have been found in our solar system. The first scientist to discover moons around another planet was the Italian astronomer Galileo Galilei. In 1609, he used a spyglass to observe the night sky. Galileo saw what looked like four stars around Jupiter, but he soon realized they were moons.

Many moons are similar to Earth in size and shape, but they can also be smaller, larger, or different shapes. Some have atmospheres, volcanoes, or frozen oceans. Most are too small to have enough gravity to hold an atmosphere, but Saturn's largest moon, Titan, is an exception. Its atmosphere is denser than Earth's.

Most scientists think our moon formed during an event called the big splash. According to this theory, a Mars-size object smashed into Earth. The impact created broken pieces of debris, and when gravity brought them together, they formed the moon. This would explain why some rocks on the moon and Earth share similar characteristics. Massive collisions in space may

AN ARTIST'S ILLUSTRATION SHOWS THE BIG SPLASH, WHEN AN OBJECT SMASHED INTO EARTH. THE DEBRIS FORMED THE MOON.

have formed other moons, too. Some moons in our solar system may be objects that escaped the Kuiper belt or Oort cloud.

The Latin word for moon is *luna*. The word "lunar" describes things related to the moon—like a lunar crater. It is also the root of "lunatic" and "loony"—words that arose from the superstition that people behave strangely during a full moon.

Megahot Mercury

Mercury is a record setter in the solar system. It is the closest planet to the sun, at an average distance of 36 million miles (58 million km). It travels around the sun faster than any of the other planets, and its orbit is more egg-shaped. Just slightly larger than Earth's moon, Mercury is the smallest planet in the solar system. A terrestrial planet, it has a giant iron core and a strong magnetic field, but no moons of its own. Mercury spins so slowly, it takes 59 Earth days to complete one turn, meaning one day on Mercury equals 59 days on Earth. Its slow

TO BE OR NOT TO BE ... A PLANET

WHAT IS A PLANET, ANYWAY? You might have heard what happened to Pluto. It was considered a planet until 2006, when the International Astronomical Union defined a planet as an object that can do three things:

1. Orbit the sun
2. Form a round or nearly round shape
3. Have gravity strong enough to clear away nearby objects

Even though Pluto was considered a planet for 76 years after its discovery in 1930, the new definition meant it needed a new name. Now Pluto is called a dwarf planet because its gravity is too weak to draw in or sling away nearby celestial objects.

HELLO, PLUTO! THIS PHOTO WAS TAKEN BY NASA'S NEW HORIZONS SPACECRAFT IN 2015.

spin and short year mean it takes a long time for the sun to appear in the same place in Mercury's sky. For this reason, the sun only rises about every 176 Earth days.

A Mercury year lasts 88 Earth days. If you were a Mercuryling, instead of an Earthling, you could celebrate your birthday every three months! Unfortunately, living on Mercury would never work. It is the second hottest planet in the solar system, with temperatures reaching 800°F (427°C) during the day and minus 290°F (-178°C) at night. Its atmosphere is too weak to hold in daytime heat. No other planet's temperature shifts this much. Solar winds constantly blow over Mercury's rocky, crater-covered surface, and its atmosphere is thinner than that of any other planet in the solar system—another record! It also has weak gravity. If your weight is 100 pounds (45 kg) on Earth, you would weigh 38 pounds (17 kg) on Mercury.

A DIFFERENT LOOK AT MERCURY: THE COLORS IN THIS IMAGE REPRESENT THE VARIOUS QUALITIES OF THE ROCKS THAT MAKE UP ITS SURFACE.

The Oddball, Venus

Venus is the second planet from the sun, the second largest terrestrial planet, and Earth's closest neighbor. Yellowish sulfuric acid clouds surround it, reflecting the sun's light and making Venus the brightest object in the night sky after the moon. If you could peek through its yellowish clouds, you would spot craters, volcanoes, and lava plains, but no water. One mountain range on Venus is taller than Mount Everest!

Sometimes called Earth's sister, Venus is only a bit smaller in size and mass than Earth. However, Venus doesn't have any moons, its magnetic field is weak, and its climate is very different from ours. The cloud layers and plentiful carbon dioxide in the atmosphere trap the sun's heat like a thick quilt, creating a greenhouse effect that makes the temperature soar. Even though Venus averages 67 million miles (108 million km) from the sun, it is even hotter than Mercury. The temperature—hot enough to melt lead—reaches 880°F (471°C). Even if it didn't have such extreme temperatures, you could not visit Venus. Acid rain falls from the clouds, and the dry air, with its rotten-egg smell, is extremely dense. Walking through it would feel like pushing through water.

In some ways, Venus is a bit of an oddball. It rotates in the opposite direction from all the other planets, except Uranus. It's believed a collision with another planetary-size object, early in Venus's history, caused it to spin differently. Its backward rotation makes the sun rise in the west and set in the east. Also, it turns slowly, taking 243 Earth days to complete one rotation. Since Venus takes 225 Earth days to orbit the sun, its day is longer than its year.

The strength of Venus's gravity is close to Earth's. If you weigh 100 pounds (45 kg) on Earth, you would weigh 91 pounds (41 kg) on Venus.

A REPRESENTATION OF VENUS'S SURFACE WAS CREATED BY MAPPING DATA FROM A NUMBER OF MISSIONS.

Home Sweet Home, Our Planet Earth

Even though Earth, the third planet from the sun, has always been your home, you might still find it holds surprises. For example, you might not have known you're traveling through space at 19 miles a second (30 km/s) as Earth orbits the sun. You are also spinning with Earth as it turns on its axis at 1,000 miles an hour (1,600 km/h) at the Equator. The force of its rotation makes the planet bulge at the Equator, unlike slow-spinning Mercury and Venus, which are almost perfectly round. A person standing on Earth's Equator is about 13 miles (21 km) farther from the planet's center than someone standing at the North Pole. Every 10 years, the bulge gets almost a third of an inch (8 mm) bigger, as Earth's motion sends melting ice in Greenland and Antarctica toward the Equator.

THERE'S NO PLACE LIKE OUR HOME PLANET! THE GREENS AND BLUES OF EARTH ARE BRIGHT IN NORTH QUEENSLAND, AUSTRALIA.

The largest terrestrial planet, Earth is the only place in the universe known to support life. How did we get so lucky? First of all, Earth has a magnetic field, thanks to its iron core. Along with the atmosphere, the magnetic field provides protection from space radiation. Earth can also support life because its atmosphere contains 21 percent oxygen, as well as carbon dioxide and other heat-trapping gases that keep the planet from getting too cold. Along with carbon, liquid water is a key ingredient for life. The first life on Earth came from the oceans. Earth's distance to the sun—called one astronomical unit (AU)—places us in the habitable zone, a region in space where the temperature is not too hot or too cold.

Earth is the only planet in the solar system with just one natural satellite, the moon. The fifth largest moon in the solar system, it orbits Earth

UNDER YOUR FEET

EARTH'S LAYERS, FROM CORE TO CRUST

EARTH IS MADE UP OF FOUR LAYERS. The crust, where you live, is the thinnest, while the mantle below it—a hot layer with the ability to flow—is the largest. Liquid metal moving inside Earth's two hottest layers—the outer and inner cores—form electric currents. These currents, along with Earth's rotation, help create the magnetic field, which protects our planet from solar and cosmic radiation.

- **CRUST:** Silicate rock 18.5–50 miles (30–80 km) thick on continents and about 0–6 miles (0–10 km) thick below oceans
- **MANTLE:** Mostly silicate rock about 1,170 miles (1,883 km) thick
- **OUTER CORE:** Molten nickel and iron
- **INNER CORE:** Solid nickel and iron

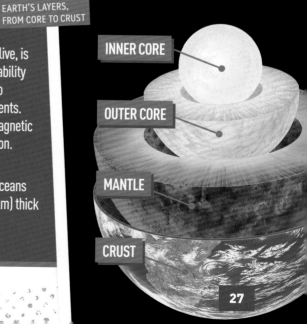

INNER CORE

OUTER CORE

MANTLE

CRUST

from an average distance of 238,855 miles (384,400 km). The moon's cratered surface contains mountains and plains, and its gravity helps cause Earth's tides. Looking up from your backyard, you can see light and dark areas on the moon's surface because of the different types, and ages, of rock there. We only see one side of the moon because its rotation and orbit rate are the same—27 days—causing the same side to always face Earth. However, because Earth is also in motion, the moon appears to orbit Earth every 29 days.

Magnificent Mars

Orbiting the sun from 142 million miles (228 million km), Mars is the last of the terrestrial planets and the second smallest planet in the solar system. The American government organization NASA (National Aeronautics and Space Administration) is exploring sending a manned mission to Mars. It will take new technologies about nine months of travel time to reach Mars.

Mars is called the red planet because of its brownish red surface. Even though Earth is bigger, the two planets have about the same amount of land because so much of Earth is underwater. The Martian landscape includes mountains, canyons, craters, plains, and dry beds from ancient lakes—all covered with dust. It's a record holder for tallest mountain in the solar system. Olympus Mons is 15 miles (24 km) high, with a diameter of about 375 miles (603 km).

It is three times higher than Mount Everest, which is 5.5 miles (9 km) above sea level.

The Martian atmosphere is 100 times thinner than Earth's. Carbon dioxide is plentiful, but the atmosphere is too thin to trap much heat, creating temperatures that range from 70°F (21°C) to minus 225°F (-143°C). Like Earth, Mars is tilted on its axis. However, because of Mars's distance from the sun, the seasons last twice as long as they do on Earth. The weather on Mars includes frost, fog, and fierce dust storms, which can last for months and cover its entire surface. If astronauts reach the red planet, they will experience days that are 24 hours and 37 minutes long (each one is called a sol), and a year that lasts 687 Earth days.

Mars is the only terrestrial planet to have two moons. Phobos and Deimos may be asteroids captured by Mars's gravity. They are some of the smallest moons in the solar system and two of the darkest objects. Black lumpy rocks that look like potatoes, the moons are covered with craters, loose rock, and dust. Scientists believe Phobos may be a collection of rock held together by gravity, rather than a solid surface.

The gravity on Mars's moons is so weak, one jump would send a visitor into space. Mars also has weaker gravity than Earth. An astronaut could jump three times higher on Mars, and a person weighing 100 pounds (45 kg) on Earth would weigh 38 pounds (17 kg) on the red planet.

SOJOURNER, THE MARS PATHFINDER ROVER

THE MARS PATHFINDER SENT 2.3 BILLION BITS OF INFORMATION BACK TO EARTH. THIS IS ONE OF THE MORE THAN 16,500 IMAGES IT SENT BACK.

MARS MOON FACTS

MOON NAME	PHOBOS	DEIMOS
AVERAGE DISTANCE FROM MARS	5,826 miles (9,376 km)	14,576 miles (23,458 km)
TIME TO ORBIT MARS	7.65 hours (3 times every sol)	30 hours
RADIUS	6.9 miles (11.1 km)	3.9 miles (6.2 km)

PHOBOS, PHOTOGRAPHED BY NASA'S MARS RECONNAISSANCE ORBITER

DEIMOS HAS A SMOOTH SURFACE WITH JUST A FEW IMPACT CRATERS.

Jumbo Jupiter

Jupiter, the fifth planet from the sun, lies beyond Mars and the asteroid belt. The largest planet in the solar system, it is 11 times the diameter of Earth, and a major record holder. It has the most moons, the largest oceans, and the shortest day, at nine hours and 55.5 minutes. Jupiter is also home to the biggest and most powerful storm in the solar system. The Great Red Spot is like an Earth-size hurricane that just won't quit. It has been raging for more than 300 years! Jupiter looks like a striped marble. It spins so fast that its clouds separate, creating dark and light belts. Because Jupiter is a gas giant, it has no solid surface. So, without anything in the way to slow them down, Jupiter's winds can reach up to 335 miles an hour (539 km/h). At a distance of 484 million miles (779 million km) from the sun, Jupiter takes

HEY, JUPITER! THIS COLORFUL PHOTO WAS CREATED FROM FOUR IMAGES TAKEN BY NASA'S CASSINI SPACECRAFT.

12 years to complete one orbit and is extremely cold. Temperatures average around minus 229°F (-145°C). In 1979, scientists discovered rings more than 62,137 miles (100,000 km) wide around Jupiter. The rings formed from dust that flew up from meteoroids striking nearby moons.

When the sun formed, Jupiter got most of its leftover mass. It has tens of thousands of miles of atmosphere but, again, no solid surface. Its main ingredients—hydrogen and helium gas—surround a central, Earth-size core. Scientists are trying to determine whether the core is solid or a thick, hot, rocky soup. Thermal energy, which remains from planet formation, causes high temperatures in Jupiter's core. The heat, along with atmospheric pressure, turns hydrogen gas in Jupiter's atmosphere into layers of liquid hydrogen.

Where the pressure is great enough, the gas becomes liquid metal. Jupiter has all the ingredients to ignite into a star, but it never will. Its mass is not great enough to create the pressure and temperature needed to fuse hydrogen into helium. Jupiter would have to be 80 times more massive for that to happen. For this reason, it is considered a failed star. However, its gravity is still powerful. A 100-pound (45-kg) person on Earth would weigh 252 pounds (114 kg) on Jupiter—but no crewed missions will take place there. The extreme pressures and temperatures would crush, melt, and vaporize any visitors.

Jupiter's Moon Family

Jupiter has a family of 79 natural satellites. The first four to be discovered—Io, Europa, Ganymede, and Callisto—are its largest moons. They are called the Main Group, or the Galilean satellites, honoring their discoverer, Galileo. After the planets, these four moons are some of the solar system's largest objects—even bigger than the dwarf planets.

The rest of Jupiter's satellites are much smaller. Metis, Adrastea, Amalthea, and Thebe have diameters of less than 124 miles (200 km), the distance between the cities of Los Angeles and San Diego in California. Located inside Io's orbit, they are called the inner moons, or the Amalthea group, after Amalthea, the reddest object in the solar system. The inner moons, along with the Galilean satellites, make up a group called the regular satellites. These moons have a prograde orbit—one that moves in the same direction as the rotation of the planet. The rest of Jupiter's moons, called the irregular satellites, have more distant and eccentric orbits. Much smaller than the regular satellites, they may be asteroids captured by the planet's gravity. Jupiter's smallest moon is barely a mile across.

NASA'S GALILEO SPACECRAFT TOOK THIS IMAGE OF SATURN'S MOON IO. DOTTED WITH VOLCANIC CALDERAS, IT'S THE MOST VOLCANIC OBJECT IN THE SOLAR SYSTEM.

VOYAGER 1'S IMAGES OF JUPITER AND FOUR OF ITS MOONS, ASSEMBLED INTO A COLLAGE: IO (TOP LEFT), EUROPA (CENTER), GANYMEDE (BOTTOM LEFT), AND CALLISTO (BOTTOM RIGHT)

THE GREAT RED SPOT

Stunning Saturn

Sixth from the sun, Saturn is the second largest planet in the solar system. Nine Earths, side by side, would nearly equal its diameter. Saturn is called the jewel of the solar system because of its seven spectacular rings. Each one is a collection of ringlets made of ice chunks and ice-covered rock. Most chunks range from pebble-size to car-size, but they might also be the size of a sand grain, a mountain, or something in between. The rings even contain a few small moons! If you could place the rings between Earth and the moon, they would fill the space. The rings may have formed as gas and dust created the solar system. Or they may be leftovers from broken-up moons or comets. Scientists are not yet sure.

Saturn has a fast rotation, with its day lasting only 10 hours and 42 minutes. About 8.5 times farther from the sun than Earth is, Saturn takes 29.4 Earth years to complete an orbit, and that makes for cold temperatures: minus 288°F (-178°C) at the top of its clouds. Saturn must travel 5.6 billion miles (9 billion km) to complete its year. Like Earth's, its axis is tilted, and the angle changes how the rings look to us. For half of Saturn's year, sunlight strikes the top of its rings. For the other half, the sun lights up the bottom. About every 15 years, day and night are of equal length and both hemispheres receive the same amount of light. At this time, called the equinox, the rings point directly at the sun. Sometimes, due to the positions of Earth and Saturn, we only see the rings' thin edge, and they become nearly invisible.

If you could travel toward Saturn's center, you would see a gradual change. Pressure, along with high temperatures left from Saturn's formation, turns its gases to liquids. A drop through more than 10,000 miles

AN IMAGE CREATED FROM PHOTOS TAKEN BY NASA'S CASSINI SPACECRAFT, LOOKING UP INTO SATURN'S RING PLANE

NASA'S CASSINI SPACECRAFT TOOK THIS IMAGE OF SATURN AND ITS RINGS.

THE GREAT RED SPOT CLOSE-UP: THE SPOT IS A HURRICANE THAT'S BEEN SWIRLING FOR CENTURIES.

IMAGES TAKEN FROM DIFFERENT ALTITUDES ON SATURN'S LARGEST MOON, THE PLANET-SIZE TITAN

ENCELADUS, ANOTHER OF SATURN'S MOONS, HAS A SURFACE COVERED WITH CRATERS AND RIDGES, EVIDENCE OF GEOLOGIC ACTIVITY UNDER THE MOON'S SURFACE.

(16,093 km) of clouds would bring you to a boiling liquid hydrogen layer raging with electrical currents. If you could travel to the planet's center, you would find a huge rocky core, about 15 to 20 times Earth's mass. Even though Saturn is large, it is not very dense. In fact, Saturn is so light, it would float if you could put it in a gigantic bathtub full of water. With gravity only a bit stronger than Earth's, a 100-pound (45-kg) person standing on Saturn would weigh 106 pounds (48 kg).

Saturn's Moon Family

At least 62 moons orbit Saturn. The largest—Titan—is bigger than Mercury. It is the solar system's second largest natural satellite. Unlike other moons in the solar system, Titan has clouds and a thick atmosphere, rich with nitrogen. Sometimes methane and ethane—colorless, odorless vapors—fall as rain, and Titan is the only other known object, besides Earth, where liquid exists on the surface. Two of

ONE OF SATURN'S OUTER, ASTEROID-LIKE MOONS, PHOEBE WAS PHOTOGRAPHED BY CASSINI ON A FLYBY.

Saturn's moons have environments that could support some forms of life: Titan, due to its atmosphere, and Enceladus, which spews water vapor, icy particles, and other materials from cracks in its polar regions. Several of Saturn's other moons are icy or asteroid-like objects. Smaller moons tend to orbit either very far from Saturn or near the rings. Gravity from shepherd moons—those near the rings—helps keep the rings in shape.

Sideways Uranus

Uranus was the first planet in our solar system to be discovered with a telescope. Before English astronomer William Herschel spotted it in 1781, sky watchers thought it was a dim star or comet. Instead, it turned out to be another fascinating gas giant. Uranus completes one orbit around the sun in 84 Earth years. It is surrounded by a ring system, like Saturn's but smaller, and is home to the coldest temperatures for a planet in the solar system. The surface temperature in this frozen world averages minus 357°F (-216°C). You'd be cold, too, if you lived 1.8 billion miles (3 billion km) from the sun. The distance is so great, sunlight takes two hours and 40 minutes to reach Uranus.

Uranus is called an ice giant because ice lies below its gas. It has no solid surface, and its upper atmosphere contains hydrogen, helium, and a small amount of methane. The methane scatters blue light, giving Uranus its pale blue-green color. A mixture of ices—water, methane, and ammonia—surrounds its small rocky core.

A day on Uranus lasts about 17 hours. Like Venus, the planet rotates east to west. But unlike all the other planets, Uranus is tilted almost 98 degrees. It rotates on its side, like a top that has fallen over but keeps on spinning. One theory suggests that soon after Uranus formed, an Earth-size object smashed into it, knocking the planet on its side. This unusual tilt creates strange seasons. On Earth, the sun's most direct light strikes the Equator. On Uranus, the sun's most direct light strikes the poles. During the planet's 21-year winter, it is always dark, and during the 21-year summer, it is always light. However, during the 21 years of spring and 21 years of fall, both day and night occur. The poles are both the hottest and coldest places on Uranus.

Uranus's 13 rings probably formed as moons broke apart. As pieces smashed into each other, they shattered into bits of small rock and chunks up to the size of large boulders. The rings are thin—only a few miles thick. Most are dark gray, but one has a reddish color and another is blue.

The third largest planet in our solar system, Uranus could hold 63 Earths. However, since gas and ice are not as heavy as rock, Uranus is light for its size. A person weighing 100 pounds (45 kg) on Earth would weigh 89 pounds (40 kg) on Uranus due to its weaker gravity.

URANUS'S BRIGHTEST RING

NASA'S VOYAGER 2 PHOTOGRAPHED 9 OF URANUS'S 13 RINGS IN 1986. THE RINGS ARE THE BRIGHTEST LINES IN THE IMAGE, AND THE COLORS ARE NOT TRUE TO LIFE.

A VIEW OF URANUS CREATED BY THE KECK TELESCOPE. IT SHOWS URANUS'S TILTED AXIS.

Uranus has 27 known moons, all of them small. The inner moons, closer to the planet, are about half rock and half water ice. The outer moons are probably captured asteroids, objects trapped in Uranus's gravity. Planets and their satellites have traditionally been named after characters in Greek and Roman mythology. However, thanks to modern technology, astronomers are discovering more moons, and this has created a need for more names. To solve the problem, Uranus's moons— with names like Puck, Juliet, and Umbriel—are named after characters in stories by William Shakespeare and Alexander Pope. Other satellites may now be named after Gallic, Inuit, and Norse giants and monsters.

Noble Neptune

Neptune is the eighth and most distant planet in the solar system. Dark, cold, and windy, it is smaller than Uranus—but it's still 57 times larger than Earth. Like Uranus, Neptune is both a gas giant and an ice giant. Below its atmosphere of hydrogen, helium, and methane lie ices of water, methane, and ammonia. Neptune is a vivid blue, thanks to the methane in its atmosphere. Scientists think an extremely hot ocean may lie below its clouds. Neptune does not have a solid surface, but it does have a solid Earth-size center. It is a superstormy planet, with winds that blow clouds of frozen methane 1,200 miles an hour (1,931 km/h). Extremely cold, its temperatures average around minus 353°F (-214°C). A day lasts 16 hours and seven minutes, but its year is much longer:

NEPTUNE, ROMAN GOD OF THE SEA, INSPIRED THE NAME OF THE BLUE PLANET.

Neptune takes 165 Earth years to go around the distant sun—which is 2.8 million miles (4.5 million km) away. If you lived there, you would never even have a first birthday!

Neptune's five known rings are made of small rocks and particles of dust. In some places, dust clumps together. These thicker parts are called arcs. Dark and narrow, the rings do not form continuous circles and are not visible using amateur telescopes. Each ring is named after one of the astronomers who made a Neptunian discovery: Galle, Le Verrier, Lassell, Arago, and Adams.

While Neptune has 13 known moons, scientists are trying to confirm whether another one may exist. Its largest moon, Triton, is the only large moon in the solar system with a retrograde orbit—one that travels in the opposite direction from the planet's rotation. Part of Triton's surface looks like the skin of a cantaloupe because of volcanic

NASA'S VOYAGER 2 SNAPPED THIS IMAGE OF NEPTUNE FROM 4.4 MILLION MILES (7 MILLION KM) AWAY.

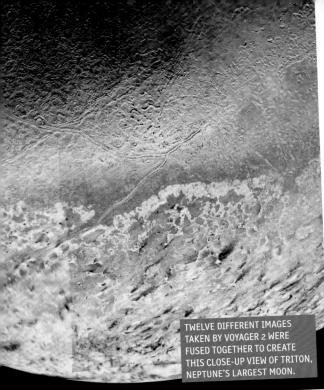

TWELVE DIFFERENT IMAGES TAKEN BY VOYAGER 2 WERE FUSED TOGETHER TO CREATE THIS CLOSE-UP VIEW OF TRITON, NEPTUNE'S LARGEST MOON.

AN ARTIST'S ILLUSTRATION SHOWS WHAT THE SURFACE OF AN ICY, FARAWAY BODY CALLED A KUIPER BELT OBJECT MIGHT LOOK LIKE.

emissions—mainly nitrogen gas and solid particles that rise above the surface and into the very thin atmosphere. Much of that material spreads downwind from volcanoes, forming darker deposits. Its volcanoes and geysers also spew ices into the air. Cryovolcanoes—or ice volcanoes—are mountains formed of frozen liquids. They spew water, methane gas, ammonia, and carbon dioxide in the form of liquids, slush, ice, or vapors.

Kuiper Belt

Beyond Neptune, a giant ring of icy bodies, called the Kuiper belt, orbits the sun. It was named after Dutch-American scientist George Kuiper, who wanted to explain where comets and other icy objects came from. In 1951, he wondered if a belt of icy objects existed beyond Neptune, but they were hard to spot. Finally, in 1992, telescopes located an object that was eventually named Albion. More discoveries followed, and

eventually, the region was recognized to be a disk of icy objects 2.3 billion miles (3.7 billion km) wide. Kuiper was proved right.

Kuiper belt objects (KBOs) look like faint stars. They orbit the sun in an area that begins in Neptune's orbit at about 30 AU and reaches to 50 AU. The Kuiper belt is where you will find dwarf planets like Pluto, Eris, Haumea, and Makemake, as well as Halley's comet and other short-period comets—those that orbit the sun in less than 200 years. The belt is home to rock and ice, with some chunks as small as an ice cube and others more than 62 miles (100 km) in diameter. Most KBOs, however, range from 6 to 31 miles (10 to 50 km) across. The Kuiper belt may contain more than a trillion comets. Objects with orbits beyond Neptune are also called trans-Neptunian objects. Additional objects are found in a region called the scattered disk. Overlapping the outer edge of the main part of the Kuiper belt, it extends to almost 1,000 AU.

POSSIBLE PLANET NINE

COULD THERE BE A NINTH PLANET IN OUR SOLAR SYSTEM? Astronomers gather clues on a possible Planet Nine by watching how distant objects in space behave. Another planet would explain why some Kuiper belt objects have such stretched-out orbits. Using math, models, and computer simulations, astronomers try to predict what Planet Nine might be like and where it might be found. If it exists, it's probably a Neptune-size object. It is believed to lie far beyond Pluto, which means it would take 10,000 to 20,000 Earth years to go around the sun. That's about 20 times the orbit of Neptune. Astronomers use telescopes to look for Planet Nine, but—if it exists—this faint, faraway object is hard to spot!

Dwarf Planets and Beyond

In addition to the terrestrial planets and gas and ice giants, the solar system is dotted with dwarf planets and other objects. Here's a closer look at a few of the better-known ones.

Pint-Size Pluto

Pluto is famous! First a planet, now a dwarf planet, it is one of the larger objects in the Kuiper belt, and the brightest when viewed from Earth. Pluto is not like the eight planets in our solar system. Instead of lying in the same plane, its orbit tilts 57 degrees. Pluto travels in a path so eccentric, it is sometimes closer to us than Neptune! Its journey around the sun takes 248 years, and each day lasts about 6.4 Earth days. It rotates on its side, like Uranus, and spins backward—east to west. That makes the sun rise in the west and set in the east, the opposite of what happens on Earth. A mysterious world with blue skies, high mountains, and extreme cold, Pluto has a surface temperature that can be minus 375 to minus 400°F (-226 to -240°C). It is a rocky, icy object that's smaller than Earth's moon, yet it

AN IMAGE OF PLUTO CREATED FROM NASA'S NEW HORIZONS SPACECRAFT AND OTHER INSTRUMENTS SHOWS AN AREA ON ITS SURFACE CALLED THE HEART. CAN YOU SPOT IT?

AN ARTIST'S ILLUSTRATION OF PLANET NINE SHOWS FLASHES OF LIGHTNING ON ITS SURFACE, AND THE SUN AS A DISTANT DOT.

A SCIENTIFIC ILLUSTRATION OF ODDLY SHAPED HAUMEA SHOWS ITS MOONS, HI'IAKA AND NAMAKA.

has five moons of its own. Its largest, Charon, is about half Pluto's size. Pluto's other moons are called Kerberos, Styx, Nix, and Hydra.

Ceres

Ceres is a dwarf planet named after the ancient Roman goddess of harvests. Like Pluto, it was reclassified. Astronomers used to call moonless Ceres an asteroid, but it is not like most asteroids. It is larger and spherical, and it orbits the sun. The biggest object in the asteroid belt, with a diameter of 590 miles (950 km), Ceres makes up 25 percent of the asteroid belt's mass.

CERES, THE ROMAN GOD OF HARVESTS

Makemake

Makemake (MAH-keh-MAH-keh) is the second brightest KBO. Slightly smaller than Pluto, it has a reddish surface covered with frozen ethane, methane, and nitrogen. Its one moon is small—only 100 miles (161 km) in diameter. Makemake was given the nickname "Easterbunny" after its discovery close to Easter in 2005.

Haumea

Observations in 2003 and 2004 led to the discovery of football-shaped Haumea (how-MAY-uh). Nicknamed "Santa" because it was detected close to Christmas, Haumea tumbles through the Kuiper belt, end over end. One of the solar system's fastest-rotating large objects, Haumea spins so fast, its day lasts only four hours. It has two moons: Namaka and Hi'iaka. A rocky object coated with thin ice, Haumea is the third brightest KBO.

Eris

The discovery of Eris, as well as Makemake, made scientists question the definition of a planet (See To Be or Not To Be ... a Planet, page 25). Close in size to Pluto, Eris has a gigantic orbit that takes it out of the Kuiper belt during its 557-year path around the sun. When it's far from the sun, its atmosphere freezes and falls to the ground as snow. Eris has one moon, Dysnomia.

DWARF PLANET ERIS MAY HAVE A FROST-COVERED SURFACE, AS PICTURED IN THIS SCIENTIFIC DRAWING.

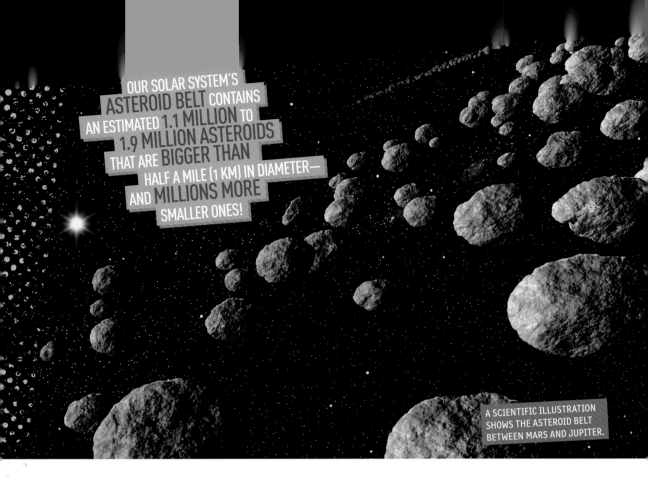

OUR SOLAR SYSTEM'S ASTEROID BELT CONTAINS AN ESTIMATED 1.1 MILLION TO 1.9 MILLION ASTEROIDS THAT ARE BIGGER THAN HALF A MILE (1 KM) IN DIAMETER—AND MILLIONS MORE SMALLER ONES!

A SCIENTIFIC ILLUSTRATION SHOWS THE ASTEROID BELT BETWEEN MARS AND JUPITER.

Asteroid Belt

Small rocky objects that orbit the sun are called asteroids. You might think of them as planetary leftovers. When Jupiter formed, leftover objects smashed into each other, breaking into fragments that became asteroids. A few are spherical, but most have jagged, irregular shapes, and surfaces with pits and craters. Asteroids are sometimes called minor planets. They may contain iron, nickel, or other metals. No two are alike.

Asteroids follow elliptical paths around the sun, rotating as they go. Those with uneven shapes may tumble along, a bit like a poorly thrown football. Sometimes asteroids crash into each other. They may break apart, forming smaller rock fragments called meteoroids.

If you could put all the asteroids in our solar system together, they would equal less than half the mass of the moon. Most are found in the asteroid belt, between Mars and Jupiter. The belt stretches across a region as wide as the distance between the sun and Earth. Most of these asteroids—up to 1.9 million—are bigger than 0.6 mile (1 km) in diameter. Millions of smaller ones exist, too. More than 150 asteroids are known to have a moon. Some even have two moons!

Every year, more asteroids are discovered. Some are found outside the asteroid belt. Those that share their orbits with a planet are called trojans. Jupiter, Neptune, Mars, Saturn, and Earth all have trojan asteroids. Earth's trojan is 50 million miles (80 million km) away and will never collide with our planet. Asteroids that do come closer are called near-Earth asteroids. Scientists watch the skies for such objects and explore ways to prevent an impact.

The Oort Cloud

The Oort cloud is a group of icy objects believed to circle the entire solar system—but no one can say for sure if the Oort cloud exists. At least not yet.

Imagine being inside an enormous glass ball. The sun is at the center, and the ball is made of icy objects that circle it. The objects may be mountain-size or even larger, orbiting at more than a light-year from the sun.

Scientists suggest gravity from a star can tug an Oort object and pull it into the inner solar system. When this happens, a new comet is born! These objects, called long-period comets, have giant orbits that can take more than 200 years to complete. Long-period comets, like Hale-Bopp (1995) and Hyakutake (1996), are tough to study. Most of the time, they are too far away.

The Oort cloud is named for Dutch astronomer Jan Oort (rhymes with "port"). In 1950, Oort suggested that an icy sphere around the solar system would explain where long-period comets come from. No one can say for sure if the Oort cloud exists. At least, not yet!

THE BLUE SPHERE REPRESENTS WHAT THE OUTER OORT CLOUD MIGHT LOOK LIKE.

THE VAN ALLEN BELTS, SHOWN IN THIS ILLUSTRATION IN YELLOW AND THE SPACES BETWEEN THEM IN GREEN, ARE CREATED BY EARTH'S MAGNETOSPHERE.

Van Allen Belts

Did you know you live on a giant magnet? Deep in Earth's iron and nickel core, the moving liquid metal generates electric currents, which produce magnetic fields. Earth's magnetic field, called the magnetosphere, stretches into space. The magnetosphere traps plasma, which forms two enormous regions beyond Earth's atmosphere called the Van Allen belts. Like our atmosphere, the belts are invisible. If you could see them, it would look a bit like Earth has two giant ears.

The smaller, inner belt stretches from 400 to 6,000 miles (644 to 9,656 km) above our planet. The larger, outer belt extends from 8,400 to 36,000 miles (13,518 to 57,936 km). Their sizes swell and shrink, depending on how much energy the sun releases. Sometimes the outer radiation belt seems to split in two, and so a third belt was observed for four weeks in 2013. It disappeared due to an interplanetary shock wave, something that can occur as fast streams of solar wind catch up to slower streams and create sudden changes in flow. Like a giant broom, the fast solar wind sweeps up the slower wind, creating a dense region ahead of it. When this and other eruptions from the sun strike Earth, they cause space storms, which sometimes destroy the third belt. James Van Allen, a University of Iowa physicist, discovered the Van Allen belts in 1958. It's not easy to study what you can't see. Information collected from instruments on Explorer 1, the first United States satellite, helped him build his theory, which another satellite—Explorer 3—later confirmed.

NUCLEUS: ICY CHUNK OF ROCK AND ICE.

ION TAIL: A THINNER, STRAIGHTER TAIL THAT CONTAINS GAS THAT IS IONIZED—MEANING GAS ATOMS HAVE GAINED OR LOST ELECTRONS.

DUST TAIL: GAS AND DUST ARE PUSHED AROUND THE COMA, CAUSING VERY TINY DUST PARTICLES TO FORM A BROAD TAIL THAT CAN REACH UP TO 60 MILLION MILES (97 MILLION KM) LONG.

COMA: CLOUD THAT FORMS AROUND THE NUCLEUS AS THE COMET MOVES TOWARD THE SUN, CREATED FROM DUST AND MELTING ICE AS IT BOILS INTO A GAS.

A COMET SPEEDS THROUGH SPACE.

Comets and Meteoroids

Made up of frozen rock, dust, and gases, comets are sometimes called dirty snowballs. Like asteroids, they orbit the sun. But while asteroids are mostly rock, comets are mostly frozen water, methane, or ammonia. A comet's center, called the nucleus, can be nearly six miles (10 km) wide—the size of a small town.

Comets have elongated orbits that take them both near and very far from the sun. As a comet gets close to the sun's heat, its shape begins to change. Frozen gases thaw and escape the dirty snowball. Dust particles, smaller than a grain of sand, escape, too. The nucleus looks like a glowing ball as dust and gas stream out and make a tail that stretches millions of miles into space. When the comet gets farther from the sun, its tail disappears and the nucleus freezes solid again.

Leftovers from when the sun, planets, and moon formed, comets contain materials that can help scientists understand how the solar system came to exist. Most comets, however, are too far away to see. Some crash into the sun. Others break apart because of the sun's gravity. Some comets have such long orbits, we may see them once but never again. Others swing by every few years. Halley's comet, which has a nucleus of 10 x 5 x 5 miles (16 x 8 x 8 km), passes by Earth about every 76 years. When it gets close to the sun, about 6.5 yards (6 m) of ice and dust stream out from its nucleus.

COMET HYAKUTAKE WAS DISCOVERED IN 1996. SCIENTISTS EXPECT THAT THE NEXT TIME THE COMET PASSES THIS CLOSE TO EARTH WILL BE IN 14,000 YEARS.

THE GEMINID METEOR SHOWER RAINS DOWN AT ITS PEAK IN MID-DECEMBER.

Loads of Meteoroids

When the solar system formed, so did dust particles and small rock chunks called meteoroids. Some meteoroids come from comets or asteroids that smashed into one another.

Every day, at least 100 tons (90 t) of dust and sand-size particles approach Earth from space. When these objects enter Earth's atmosphere, they are called meteors. They burn up as they travel through the atmosphere, creating a jolt of light that quickly disappears. People like to call them "shooting," or "falling," stars.

Most space rocks are about the size of peas, but bigger ones can occur. Large meteors, known as fireballs, create the brightest streaks of light.

Space rocks that reach Earth's surface are meteorites. Since so much of Earth is covered with water, most fall into the ocean.

LIGHTS THAT DANCE

AURORAS ARE STREAMS OF LIGHT that ripple across the sky like a beautiful light show in space. They occur as solar winds become more forceful. When a storm called a coronal mass ejection (CME) occurs, powerful eruptions on the sun send high-speed streams of energetic particles toward Earth. They reach Earth's magnetosphere after one to three days and follow the magnetic field to the North and South Poles. The sun's particles strike gases, like oxygen and nitrogen, in Earth's atmosphere. When this happens, the gases release energy, which we see as stunning auroras that dance across the sky. The lights may be green, white, red, blue, or purple, depending on what type of gas the sun's particles strike. Auroras occur on other planets, too, like Saturn and Jupiter.

THE AURORA BOREALIS GLOWS ABOVE TROMSØ, NORWAY.

SPACE WATCH: SPOT A METEOR!

If you watch the sky on a moonless night, you might see half a dozen meteors an hour— even more between midnight and dawn. The best way to see meteors is to watch during a meteor shower. They occur every year, at the same time, as Earth passes through trails of comet debris. During a shower, you might spot between 20 to 50 meteors an hour.

Each meteor shower appears to come from one area of the sky, called its radiant. The showers are named after the constellation where they appear to originate, but the constellation name just describes an area of sky—it's not the shower's source, and you can spot meteors in different parts of the sky.

The schedule here gives the peak dates for major showers, but check a local newspaper or search online for "meteor shower" and your location to find out the best dates for your area. They change every year, due to Earth's orbit and rotation. Also, look up a calendar for moon phases for the best time of night for viewing. If possible, choose a moonless night.

1. Check the meteor shower schedule.
2. Locate the constellation that gives the shower its name.
3. Choose a safe, dark location, and dress for the weather.
4. Give your eyes time to get used to the dark.
5. Look up!

THE PERSEID METEORS ZOOM AGAINST THE MILKY WAY.

MORE PERSEIDS!

NAME	WHEN TO WATCH EVERY YEAR	APPROX. METEORS (PER HOUR AT PEAK)	CONSTELLATION	VISIBILITY	
QUADRANTIDS (Shower is named after an old constellation: Quadrans Muralis.)	December 28– January 12	80	BOÖTES near the end of the Big Dipper's handle	Best views are in Northern Hemisphere	WINTER
LYRIDS	April 21–22	20	LYRA the Harp	Best views are in Northern Hemisphere	SPRING
ETA AQUARIDS	April 19– May 8	10–20	AQUARIUS the Water Carrier	Both hemispheres	SPRING
DELTA AQUARIDS	July 12– August 23	20	AQUARIUS the Water Carrier	Southern Hemisphere and southern latitudes of Northern Hemisphere	SUMMER
PERSEIDS	July 14– August 24	Up to 100	PERSEUS the Hero	Northern Hemisphere	SUMMER
ORIONIDS	October 2– November 7	15	ORION the Hunter	Both hemispheres	FALL
TAURIDS	September– November	5	TAURUS the Bull	Both hemispheres	FALL
LEONIDS	November 6–30	15	LEO the Lion	Both hemispheres	FALL
GEMINIDS	December 4–17	120	GEMINI the Twins	Both hemispheres	FALL

FLASHLIGHT

SEEING IN THE DARK

IT'S HARD FOR YOUR EYES TO GO BACK AND FORTH between light and dark. You will see a lot more in the night sky if you give your eyes at least 30 minutes to get used to the dark (40 minutes is even better). Avoid using white light. If you need to use light in the dark, make it red. You can cover a flashlight with something see-through and red, like a sheer red fabric. The red hue will allow you to see without ruining your night vision.

SPACE LAB

GRAVITY GAMES

Gravity is an important force that makes the universe exist as we know it. Without it, you would float away, and the planets would not orbit the sun. Legend says Sir Isaac Newton "discovered" gravity when an apple fell on his head. While he may have simply observed an apple falling from a tree, he did define the universal law of gravitation. It states that two objects will exert a gravitational force on one another.

EXPERIMENT LIKE SIR ISAAC NEWTON!

What you need:

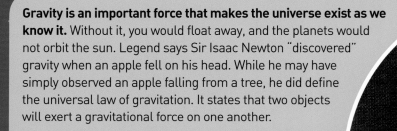

PEN

PAPER CUP

STOOL

SINK

What to do:

1. **Use the pen to punch a small hole in the side of the cup,** about an inch (2.5 cm) up from the bottom.

2. **Plug the outside of the hole with one thumb,** and fill the cup with water.

3. **Try to predict what will happen if you remove your thumb.** Now, remove your thumb.

4. **Use your thumb to reseal the hole, and refill the cup with water.** Try to predict what the water will do if you drop the cup.

5. **Step on the stool, hold the cup high,** and drop it into the sink.

WATER SPILLS OUT THROUGH THE HOLE.

What's Happening

Think of the cup as a small environment. When you uncovered the hole the first time, gravity pulled water from the environment. When you released the entire cup, the water traveled at the same rate as the cup, so it did not pour out the hole. The falling cup of water experiences a brief few seconds of weightlessness because the cup and water fall together at the same rate.

When the International Space Station orbits Earth, weightlessness occurs because the station and everyone in it are falling around Earth at the same speed. The weightlessness is called microgravity because gravity's pull is so weak.

ASTRONAUTS FLOAT IN THE KIBO LABORATORY ON THE INTERNATIONAL SPACE STATION IN 2010.

USING SPECIAL EQUIPMENT CALLED A WIDE FIELD CAMERA 3/UVIS DETECTOR, SCIENTISTS CAN CAPTURE HIGH-RESOLUTION IMAGES, LIKE THIS ONE OF A STELLAR JET GLOWING IN THE CARINA NEBULA, ALMOST 8,500 LIGHT-YEARS AWAY.

CHAPTER 2

BEYOND OUR SOLAR SYSTEM

INTRODUCTION

FOR AN ASTRONOMER, BEING "IN THE FIELD" MEANS TRAVELING

to observatories to collect data on stars, planets, galaxies, asteroids, and more. Telescopes are built in remote locations, far away from the light pollution of cities.

MUNAZZA ALAM

They are in some of the highest and driest places on Earth. It's always an interesting experience to use telescopes. When I go observing, I rest as much as possible during the day so that I can stay up all night to work!

If you've ever set up a telescope in your backyard, you may have looked through its eyepiece to observe stars or planets. When I'm at the telescope, I'm not looking through an eyepiece. Instead, I hang out in the telescope control room, which houses several computers that tell the telescope where to point. I can control the position and movement of the telescope with them.

In the control room, I am usually accompanied by a telescope operator, someone who is trained in how to use the telescope as well as troubleshoot, in case something goes wrong. I set up my observations, and the telescope operator moves the telescope to focus on my targets. To make sure everything goes smoothly, I prepare ahead of time by planning what to observe and when.

Taking observations is hard work, and sometimes I get hungry! In the middle of the night, I eat a "night lunch"—usually a sandwich and some snacks. I also drink a cup of tea or coffee to help me stay awake.

There is always a bit of luck involved in observing, because being able to get good observations depends on the weather. Sometimes you wait at the telescope all night, but if it's too cloudy or rainy you won't get any observing done.

If the weather conditions aren't right for observing, I try to stay busy by playing games or music, or visiting observers at other telescopes. I always keep my fingers crossed for clear skies when I'm headed to the telescope!

MUNAZZA FLICKS THE SWITCH TO BEGIN CALIBRATIONS USING THE MAGELLAN 1 BAADE TELESCOPE BEFORE A NIGHT OF OBSERVING.

RESEARCHERS SLEEP ALL DAY SO THEY CAN WORK ALL NIGHT MAKING ASTRONOMICAL OBSERVATIONS.

MAGELLANIC CLOUDS

THE MAGELLAN 1 BAADE TELESCOPE SCANS THE SKIES AT THE LAS CAMPANAS OBSERVATORY IN CHILE.

STARS BEGIN AS COOL CLOUDS OF GAS AND TAKE HUNDREDS OF THOUSANDS OF YEARS TO FORM.

Every day, about 275 million stars are born, and the same number die, somewhere in the observable universe.

Stars Under Construction

How do those twinkles of light in the dark sky come to be? Stars are born in giant clouds of gas and dust called nebulae. A nebula can be many light-years across and contain enough matter to make several thousand sun-size stars. A nebula is mostly hydrogen and helium, with just one percent of its mass made up of dust. Over millions of years, a nebula shrinks as gravity draws gas and dust together into clumps. As a clump grows denser, its gravity becomes stronger, causing the mass to spin. Just as figure skaters spin faster by pulling in their arms, a nebula spins faster as it comes together. The core collapses faster than the rest of the clump, and this makes it twirl ever faster. Hydrogen atoms collide with one another, making the nebula grow hotter and hotter. Eventually, the clump collapses under its own gravity, breaking into smaller pieces that

A PROTOSTAR IS BORN FROM A SWIRLING NEBULA OF GAS AND DUST. NASA RESEARCHERS NICKNAMED THIS ONE "THE TADPOLE."

collapse, too. A protostar—the hot, dense cloud of gas that collapses to form a star—forms at the center of each cloud as matter is drawn into a ball. After a few million years, protostars become young stars called T Tauri stars. They look a lot like main sequence stars—stars that convert hydrogen to helium, like our sun. But a nuclear reaction does not make them shine. Instead, T Tauri stars shine by releasing energy as they collapse. It can take from 100,000 to 10 million years for a protostar to become a main sequence star. The color it becomes will depend on its temperature, and its temperature will depend on its mass.

Main Sequence Stars

Most stars—90 percent—are main sequence stars. To enter the main sequence stage, a T Tauri star must get hot enough for nuclear fusion to occur. It begins when the star's core reaches 27 million degrees Fahrenheit (15 million degrees Celsius). As hydrogen converts into helium, the glowing star contracts as gravity tries to pull material in but the powerful nuclear reaction pushes outward. The forces balance out, and the star becomes stable. Main sequence stars release vast amounts of energy. Heat, light, and x-rays and other radiation will stream out for a very long time. The star's life span depends on its mass. Sun-size stars emit energy for 10 to 15 billion years. More massive stars are hotter and may burn through their material faster, lasting from only a few million to a few billion years.

Main sequence stars that shine steadily—like our sun—are called normal stars. They may be

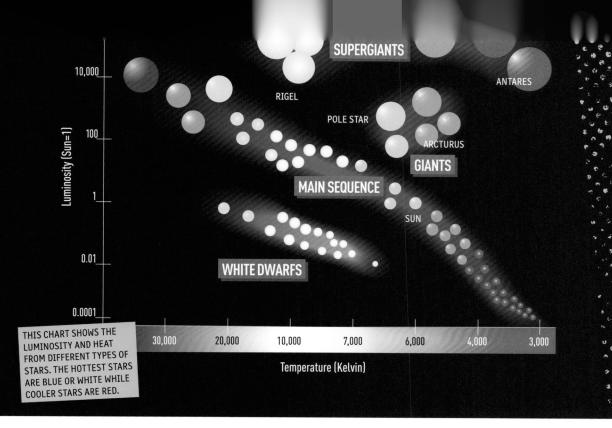

red, orange, yellow, white, or blue, depending on their temperature. (Blue is the hottest and red is the coolest.) Most are smaller than our sun, but some are the same size or bigger. Even though the sun is "normal," it is not typical. Most stars have companion stars and some are part of clusters, but our sun is all alone. Other stars, called abnormal stars, include giant, dwarf, and variable stars.

Giant Stars

In the last stages of its life cycle, a main sequence star grows into a red giant. This happens when a star's hydrogen begins to run out. Without fuel, the nuclear reaction stops, and gravity becomes the stronger force. The core collapses and the star's outer hydrogen shell puffs out, making the star grow larger. It is a giant! Now 1,000 to 10,000 times brighter, the star is also a different color. Billions of years from now, our sun will become a red giant. Its layers will reach Mercury and Venus, and may engulf Earth. Our sun will spend about a billion years as a red giant, fusing helium in its core into carbon. What happens next depends on the star's mass. A low-mass star, like our sun, will become a white dwarf, then a black dwarf. A high-mass star—one with a mass 10 times greater than our sun—will become a

BETELGEUSE, A GIANT STAR, IS ONE OF THE BIGGEST STARS FOUND SO FAR IN SPACE. ITS DIAMETER IS ABOUT 700 TIMES LARGER THAN OUR SUN'S!

WHITE DWARF

WHEN NEUTRON STARS COLLIDE, AS SHOWN IN THIS ILLUSTRATION, THEY CAN MERGE TO FORM A BLACK HOLE.

THIS ARTWORK SHOWS A WHITE DWARF SHINING IN THE CENTER OF AN ACCRETION DISK—A RING OF ROCKS AND DEBRIS, ALL THAT'S LEFT OF THE PLANETS THAT ONCE SURROUNDED IT.

supernova, then either a neutron star or black hole. Stars with the greatest mass and size are called supergiants. Imagine a star 10 to 70 times the size of our sun. Usually red or blue, supergiants are the brightest stars because they are so big. Extremely hot, blue supergiants use their fuel fast, running out after about a few hundred million years. This is a short time compared to our sun, which will take about 11 billion years to reach the white dwarf stage.

Dwarf Stars

After about a billion years as a red giant, a star runs out of helium. It begins to burn other elements—carbon, nitrogen, and oxygen—and this burst of energy blows the star's outer hydrogen layers into space. The layers form a ring around the star's core, called a planetary

A PLANETARY NEBULA FORMS AROUND A STAR'S CORE.

nebula, so named because of its round shape, like a planet. Without fuel, a low-mass star—like our sun—collapses. Gravity brings all its matter together, forming a star about the size of Earth. It is so dense, a single teaspoon would weigh up to 110 tons (100 t). Now called a white dwarf, the star shines white until the last of its energy is used up. Over billions of years, it glows until it becomes too cool to see. The white dwarf has become a black dwarf. No black dwarfs exist, however. That's because it takes up to hundreds of billions of years for the star to cool down, and the universe isn't old enough yet to have produced a black dwarf. The oldest stars are only about 15 billion years old.

The most common stars are red dwarfs— dim main sequence stars with lower masses than our sun. Red dwarfs are not very hot, and

AN EXPLODING STAR, ALSO CALLED A SUPERNOVA, SHOOTS OUT LOADS OF ENERGY AND RADIATION. A SUPERNOVA IS THE BRIGHTEST THING WE CAN SEE IN SPACE.

that makes their hydrogen supply last longer—they burn their fuel at a slower rate. Unlike sun-size stars, red dwarfs can live for trillions of years.

Brown dwarfs are objects that are not actually stars at all. Bigger than Jupiter but smaller than a small star, they are not massive enough to create the heat needed for nuclear fusion. Brown dwarfs are sometimes called failed stars.

HERE'S A SNEAK PEEK AT A STAR JUST BEFORE IT BECOMES A SUPERNOVA.

When a Star Collapses

A massive star—larger than eight suns in mass—does not become a dwarf. Instead, it bloats into a supergiant. Its mass is so great, gravitational pressure creates core temperatures high enough to fuse heavier elements. Imagine the star's layers to be an onion, with each layer being an element that is being fused. The star burns its fuel for a few million years until its core becomes iron, which cannot fuse to form another element. With nothing left to fuse, the star only has a few days left to live. It can no longer create enough pressure to stop gravity's force. Gravity takes over, crushing the core and causing its temperature to increase by billions of degrees. It happens so fast that shock waves occur and the star becomes a supernova—an exploding star. It shoots its outer layers into space at 9,000 to 25,000 miles a second (14,500 to 40,200 km/s). This creates a brilliant display of light—the brightest space phenomenon we can see. The rest of the star is destroyed. It collapses, creating a small object about 12.5 miles (20 km) in diameter, called a neutron star.

TWO STARS ORBIT EACH OTHER IN A BINARY STAR SYSTEM.

IN APRIL 2019, RESEARCHERS COORDINATED EIGHT RADIO TELESCOPES AROUND THE GLOBE TO CREATE THIS IMAGE OF A SUPERMASSIVE BLACK HOLE AT THE CENTER OF A GALAXY NAMED MESSIER 87.

AN ARTIST'S ILLUSTRATION SHOWS A SUPERMASSIVE BLACK HOLE THAT HAS MILLIONS OF TIMES MORE MASS THAN OUR SUN.

A supernova can also occur in a binary star system (see Seeing Double on page 57). It begins as a white dwarf star steals gas and matter from its companion star. The white dwarf grows so large, pressure and high temperatures inside the star start a nuclear reaction, and the white dwarf explodes in a supernova.

Five billion times brighter than the sun, supernovae form elements like gold, silver, and nickel. In fact, they create almost all the natural elements on Earth and in the human body. The iron in your blood and the calcium that built your bones all formed in space. You truly are stardust!

Invisible Stars

How does a star become invisible? After a massive star—one that's at least three times larger than the sun—explodes in a supernova, the force of gravity crushes the star's core. In less than a second, the collapse forms a black hole—an object in which a great amount of matter is crushed into a very small spot—and its gravity is super strong. In fact, the gravity is so strong, even light will bend and disappear into the black hole. Anything in space that gets too close is drawn inside. Planets, moons, stars— nothing can escape! As more objects enter the black hole, it becomes denser, which makes its gravity grow even more powerful. The black hole brings in more gas and dust, squeezing everything in it into a smaller and smaller space.

Black holes can be as small as an atom, while larger ones, called stellar black holes, are up to 20 times more massive than the sun. The largest black holes are called supermassive. Although black holes do not have a surface, scientists discovered their existence by watching how light, gas, dust, and other objects in space behave. In 2019, a team of astronomers did something that

AN ARTIST'S ILLUSTRATION SHOWS MATTER SWIRLING TOWARD A BLACK HOLE. ONCE SOMETHING CROSSES A BLACK HOLE'S EVENT HORIZON—THE BOUNDARY AROUND A BLACK HOLE—IT WILL FALL FORWARD INTO THE SINGULARITY, OR CENTER OF THE BLACK HOLE.

had seemed impossible. After more than a decade of work to improve ways to use radio astronomy to take images, scientists captured the first pictures of a black hole, showing its silhouette.

Lucky for us, our sun is too small to become a black hole, and the closest one to Earth is around 1,600 light-years away. Even though it is impossible for you to get too close to a black hole, scientists have a theory about what would happen if you could. The process has a fancy name: spaghettification. Imagine you are heading toward a black hole, feet first. Gravity would begin to pull on your feet before your head, and that would make you stretch out like a long piece of spaghetti. Just as stretching a piece of cooked spaghetti between your hands would cause the pasta to break apart, the same thing would happen to you. After all your stretched and broken parts zoomed into the black hole, you would be smaller than an atom.

Bright Today, Dim Tomorrow

Stars spend most of their lifetimes fusing lighter elements into heavier elements. During this period, stars are stable, and their brightness stays mostly the same as the outward force of nuclear fusion balances the pull of gravity. For example, our sun's brightness is nearly always the same. But some stars grow brighter or dimmer. Called variable stars, some become bright all of a sudden, then gradually dim, only to repeat the pattern. Watching them from Earth, we might notice a cycle that lasts hours or many months. Other variable stars grow brighter and fade again just once. There are two types of variable stars—intrinsic, which means something is going on inside the star, and extrinsic, which means something is going on outside the star.

Intrinsic variable stars are caused by physical changes. A star's brightness might

SIRIUS A, THE BRIGHTEST STAR IN OUR SKY

TO FIND SIRIUS A, LOOK FOR THIS CONSTELLATION: CANIS MAJOR, THE GREAT DOG.

ON THE BRIGHT SIDE

LET'S IMAGINE FOR A MINUTE that you're at a sleepover and a friend shines a flashlight close to your face. Now imagine you're on a beach at night and see the flash of a lighthouse in the distance. Which do you think is brighter, the flashlight or the lighthouse? The flashlight might seem brighter because it's close up to you. But its "apparent" brightness is not the same as its "actual," or "absolute," brightness. If you were standing right in front of the lighthouse, its light would be much, much

WHICH SEEMS BRIGHTER—THE FLASHLIGHT OR THE LIGHTHOUSE?

brighter than your friend's flashlight.

In the same way, some stars seem brighter than others. Their brightness depends on two things: the amount of light the star releases, and the star's distance from you.

Star brightness is described with a number called magnitude. The lower the magnitude, the brighter the star. A magnitude 1 star is bright. Some stars have negative numbers, and they're even brighter. The dimmest object a person can see has an apparent magnitude of 6. Apparent magnitude describes how the star appears, while absolute magnitude describes the star's actual brightness as if seen from a distance of 32.6 light-years. The two scales are needed because faint stars that are closer to Earth can seem brighter than distant stars that are more luminous, just like the up-close flashlight and the distant lighthouse. The brightest star in our night sky, Sirius A, is nicknamed "the Dog Star" because it's in the constellation Canis Major—the Great Dog. While its apparent magnitude is -1.46, its absolute magnitude is 1.4, which means it appears brighter because it is closer, not because it puts out more light. The closest star, our sun, has an apparent magnitude of -26.72 and an absolute magnitude of 4.8.

grow or lessen because of pulsations. This means the star's surface layers expand and contract on a regular basis. It's like when you breathe. As you take in air, your lungs expand. As you exhale air, your lungs get smaller. A star that gets brighter or dimmer from pulsations is known as a pulsating variable star. And as the star grows larger and smaller, its temperature rises and cools, too. Astronomers are able to use a very important type of pulsating variable star, called a Cepheid, to measure distances to other galaxies, because Cepheids brighten and dim in a predictable pattern.

An intrinsic variable star might also change brightness because of eruptions or flaring on the star's surface. Sometimes, though, stars change in brightness because of a violent event called a cataclysmic change. A supernova is one violent event that can make a star many times brighter, for a period lasting from days to weeks.

Other times, stars are variable because of their location in space. Called an extrinsic variable star, this type of star will become dimmer when another star or a planet passes in front of it. The closer object blocks some of the light we can see, but only temporarily. One of the most common extrinsic variable stars is a result of binary stars—two stars that orbit a common center of mass. As the stars revolve around one another, they may eclipse one another's light. Hundreds of thousands of variable stars can be seen from Earth, including a handful that can be seen with the naked eye.

Seeing Double

Earth orbits a single star. But imagine if our planet orbited two stars. Telescopes show us that systems with two or more stars are common. A multiple star system is a group of stars that are close enough together to be connected by gravity. In a binary or multiple star system, two stars orbit one another around a central spot, called the center of mass or barycenter. To find a double star system, look up at the Big Dipper. The second star from the end of the handle is really two stars—the brighter Mizar and its dimmer companion, Alcor. They are called the horse and

THIS CEPHEID STAR IS ABOUT 10 TIMES MORE MASSIVE THAN OUR SUN—AND ABOUT 15,000 TIMES MORE LUMINOUS.

A CEPHEID STAR, RS PUPPIS HELPS SCIENTISTS MEASURE DISTANCES IN SPACE. IT PULSATES IN A PREDICTABLE PATTERN, GETTING BRIGHTER AND DIMMER OVER THE COURSE OF A SIX-WEEK CYCLE.

RS PUPPIS, A CEPHEID STAR

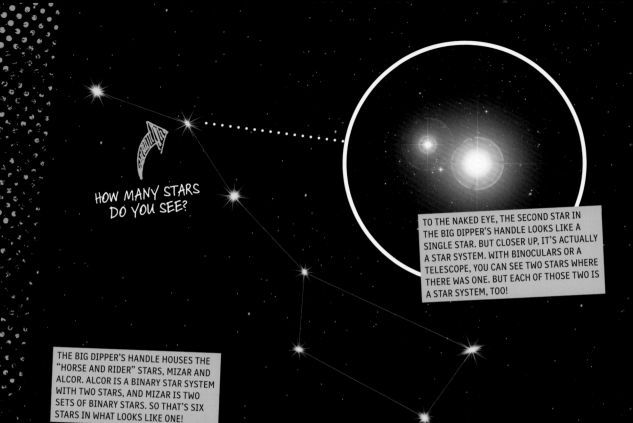

HOW MANY STARS DO YOU SEE?

TO THE NAKED EYE, THE SECOND STAR IN THE BIG DIPPER'S HANDLE LOOKS LIKE A SINGLE STAR. BUT CLOSER UP, IT'S ACTUALLY A STAR SYSTEM. WITH BINOCULARS OR A TELESCOPE, YOU CAN SEE TWO STARS WHERE THERE WAS ONE. BUT EACH OF THOSE TWO IS A STAR SYSTEM, TOO!

THE BIG DIPPER'S HANDLE HOUSES THE "HORSE AND RIDER" STARS, MIZAR AND ALCOR. ALCOR IS A BINARY STAR SYSTEM WITH TWO STARS, AND MIZAR IS TWO SETS OF BINARY STARS. SO THAT'S SIX STARS IN WHAT LOOKS LIKE ONE!

rider because it looks as though Alcor is riding Mizar. You can see them with the naked eye on a dark night. If you can't make out both stars, look through a pair of binoculars and you will see the starlight separate into two dots. Using a telescope shows you even more, for the Mizar-Alcor star system contains six stars. Alcor is a binary system, and the Mizar group contains two sets of doubles, totaling four stars. Multiple stars systems don't stop at two. If you make a wish on Polaris, the North Star, you should really get three wishes, because Polaris and its two faint companions form a triple star system.

Sometimes two stars only appear close together, but these double stars, also called optical doubles, are not part of a multiple star system. From our view on Earth, they only appear near each other. In reality, one star is far beyond the other.

Hot Jupiters

For a very long time, we knew only about the planets in our solar system. But scientists thought it seemed strange that in a universe so vast, we could belong to the only group of planets orbiting a sun. They searched the sky for many years for evidence that planets exist outside our solar system. In 1992, astronomers announced that at least two planets were orbiting a pulsar star in the constellation Virgo, but not everyone believed this kind of star could have planets. Finally, in 1995, astronomers found what they were looking for.

The first extrasolar planets, or exoplanets—planets outside our solar system—to be discovered orbiting a sun-like star were massive objects scientists called hot Jupiters. Because they are close to their stars, they are hot, and because they are mostly gas, they are like the planet Jupiter. However, with orbital periods under 10 days, they go around much more quickly. The first exoplanet—51 Pegasi b—was found near a star like our sun. About half Jupiter's size, it is 20 times closer to its star than Earth is to the sun. One orbit takes just four days. Exoplanets can exist in planetary systems very different from our own. Some systems have many hot Jupiters. Others have only a few planets that complete large orbits over hundreds of years. Some planets, like Kepler-16b, orbit two stars!

Exoplanets are hard to find. Compared to stars, planets are small. They're dim, too, because they do not make their own light—any brightness is a reflection from the stars they orbit. In fact, exoplanets can be billions of times dimmer than the stars they orbit. It is hard to spot faint objects close to a bright object, but with new technologies and methods, scientists have discovered thousands of exoplanets and continue to find more. Astronomers believe every star probably has at least one planet. So far, scientists have found that some are terrestrial but most are gas giants, Neptune-like ice giants, or super-Earths—planets with a mass larger than Earth's but smaller than Neptune's.

On March 6, 2009, NASA launched the Kepler Space Telescope. It was an exciting day—the start of the world's first mission to search for exoplanets. Up in space, Kepler focused its lens on an area of the sky with around 150,000 sun-like stars and searched for Earth-size planets orbiting stars like our sun. It located planets by watching for planetary transits—the changes in brightness that occur as a planet passes in front of its star. In the nine years it operated, Kepler found 2,343 confirmed exoplanets, mostly around distant, faint stars, and many more potential planets that astronomers are working to confirm.

AN ARTIST'S DRAWING SHOWS 51 PEGASI B, THE FIRST EXOPLANET (OR PLANET OUTSIDE OUR SOLAR SYSTEM) EVER DISCOVERED.

THE KEPLER SPACE TELESCOPE WAS LAUNCHED BY NASA IN 2009. THOUGH IT'S NO LONGER IN OPERATION, SCIENTISTS ARE STILL CONFIRMING ALL OF THE EXOPLANETS IT FOUND: 2,343 AND COUNTING.

Brighter Than a Trillion Suns

Ready for a fun word? Quasars! You can barely see them from Earth, but they are brighter than almost anything else that exists. Quasars are found in the farthest regions of the known universe. But what are they?

The detection of radio waves led to the discovery of quasars. At first, astronomers were not sure what they had found. They called their discovery quasi-stellar radio sources—quasars for short. "Quasi" is a fancy way of saying "somewhat like something," and "stellar" relates to stars. In other words, from far away, a quasar looks a bit like a star. A very bright one, in fact. Brighter than a trillion suns, quasars shoot out enormous amounts of energy. As well as light, infrared radiation, and x-rays, quasars also emit electromagnetic radiation in the form of radio waves.

Astronomers now know quasars are not stars. Exactly what they are is a puzzle, but some scientists have a theory—and it has to do with active galaxies.

NGC 1097, IN THE CONSTELLATION FORNAX, IS A SEYFERT GALAXY.

Light From Gas

The Milky Way is considered an "ordinary" or "normal" galaxy, but there are other types of galaxies, which are much less common, called active galaxies. Radio galaxies, Seyfert galaxies, quasars, and blazars are types of active galaxies. They make up a very small percentage of all the galaxies in the universe, and some are smaller than our solar system.

AN ARTIST'S ILLUSTRATION OF A QUASAR CALLED 3C 279. RESEARCHERS LINKED UP THREE RADIO TELESCOPES— IN CHILE, AND IN HAWAII AND ARIZONA, U.S.A.—TO GET A SHARP IMAGE OF 3C 279.

QUASAR 3C 279 IS FIVE BILLION LIGHT-YEARS FROM EARTH. A SUPERMASSIVE BLACK HOLE SITS AT ITS CENTER.

In a normal galaxy, most light comes from stars, and light is visible throughout the galaxy. In an active galaxy, most light comes from gas. The center glows brightest because active galaxies produce most of their radiation in the nucleus. When a galaxy emits more than 100 times the energy of the Milky Way galaxy, it is considered an active galaxy. Active galaxies are also called active galactic nuclei (AGNs).

Like other galaxies, most active galaxies have one or more supermassive black holes at their center. (Ordinary galaxies have black holes at the center, too. The Milky Way's black hole is called Sagittarius A*, or Sgr A* for short.) The black hole might be from one million to one billion solar masses—a unit of measure in which one solar mass equals the mass of the sun. It is surrounded by an accretion disk—a flat structure made up of gassy materials. Most of the disk's matter spirals into the hole, like water going down a drain. However, in active galaxies,

CENTAURUS A IS A TYPE OF GALAXY CALLED A RADIO GALAXY.

CATCH A WAVE

RADIATION IS A TYPE OF ENERGY that travels through space in waves. Radio waves are a form of electromagnetic radiation—waves that hold both an electric and magnetic field. They travel through the vacuum of space at the speed of light.

Radio waves have the longest wavelengths and vary in size from a few inches long, to several miles, to even longer than Earth. Most objects in space emit radio waves, but nebulae, quasars, pulsars, and radio galaxies emit the most.

Here on Earth, you can thank radio waves for television and radio signals. Both are artificially-made radio waves used to send information. Cell phones, cordless phones, Bluetooth, radar, and wireless computer networks use radio waves, too.

IN NEW MEXICO, U.S.A., RADIO TELESCOPES IN THE VERY LARGE ARRAY SEARCH THE SKY.

A PULSAR FLASHES EVERY FEW MILLISECONDS.

PULSARS ARE HIGHLY MAGNETIZED LEFTOVERS FROM HIGH-MASS STARS.

LITTLE GREEN MEN

TODAY WE KNOW PULSARS ARE STARS that emit flashes of light, but when they were first discovered in 1967, nobody knew what they were. Some astronomers wondered if extraterrestrials might be sending signals because the lights occurred in such a regular pattern. They called the pulsating stars LGMs—short for little green men—as a joke before discovering pulsars are a type of neutron star.

Pulsars are supermagnetic, fast-spinning leftovers from high-mass stars. Their high-energy radiation pulses are close together—only milliseconds to seconds apart. The radiation follows the pulsar's magnetic fields, speeding up and producing powerful beams of light. It is a bit like someone on a hill at night, holding a flashlight overhead and turning in circles. The light is always visible, but it is brightest when it points at you.

some of the gas evaporates and drifts away from the disk. As it does, it speeds up, almost reaching the speed of light as the black hole's rapid rotation and the disk's magnetic field squeeze the hot gas into two long jets.

The jets, which emit strong radio waves, may be hundreds of thousands of light-years long. They may even reach beyond the galaxy. Jets sometimes form objects called radio lobes, which look like giant dumbbells. These enormous regions, many twice the size of the Milky Way, emit powerful radio waves. Active galaxies can release more than 10 million times the radio energy of ordinary galaxies.

AFTER A HUGE SUPERNOVA EXPLODES, WHAT'S LEFT OVER IS ITS CORE, A NEUTRON STAR.

An active galaxy that is extremely bright is a quasar. As a quasar ages, it becomes less bright and will eventually appear as a radio galaxy or Seyfert galaxy. As even more time passes, it will become an ordinary galaxy.

Neutron Stars

While a star at least three times larger than the sun can become a black hole, a star between 1.4 and three solar masses can make the densest object in the universe—a neutron star. For a neutron star to live, a massive star must die. When the star runs out of fuel, it explodes and the core collapses. Almost all that's left is neutrons—particles with no electric charge—crushed together into a tiny, dim star. They are so dense, a piece of a neutron star the size of a sugar cube would have about the same weight as five million blue whales, or a mountain—one billion tons (900 million t). Neutron stars have magnetic fields a trillion times stronger than Earth's magnetic field. They are also the fastest spinners. While Earth takes 24 hours to complete one rotation, neutron stars might spin once per second. Some are even faster. In the second it would take you to spin around one time, some neutron stars rotate 100 times.

THIS COMPOSITE IMAGE SHOWS THE DUMBBELL-LIKE RADIO LOBES OF THE GALAXY HERCULES A.

THE BRIGHT QUASAR IN THIS IMAGE IS HE0435-1223. IT'S ONE OF THE BEST QUASAR IMAGES RESEARCHERS HAVE.

QUASAR HE0435-1223

SPACE WATCH: SPOT THESE BRIGHT STARS!

A star's brightness depends on its distance from us and its mass. Larger stars burn more brightly, but a smaller star can appear more luminous because it is closer. These bright stars are visible from both hemispheres. Here's where you can find them in the night sky.

Ursa Minor

LYRA

Hercules

BOÖTES

Coma Bere... irgo

5   VEGA

VEGA, THE FIFTH BRIGHTEST STAR IN OUR SKY, IS LOCATED IN LYRA, THE HARP.

Corona Borealis

Vulpecula

Coma Be

Delphinus

Sagitta

Serpens (Caput)

4   ARCTURUS

Corvus

Aquila

Serpens (Cauda)

Serpens

THE FOURTH BRIGHTEST STAR IN THE SKY, ARCTURUS IS LOCATED IN BOÖTES (BO-OH-TEES), THE HERDSMAN, WHICH IS SHAPED LIKE A KITE. THE STAR'S NAME IS GREEK FOR "GUARDIAN OF THE BEAR," SO NAMED BECAUSE IT IS CLOSE TO URSA MAJOR, THE GREAT BEAR, AND URSA MINOR, THE LITTLE BEAR.

Cra

Scutum

...icornus

Corvus

Sagittarius

ALPHA CENTAURI IS THE THIRD BRIGHTEST STAR IN OUR SKY AND THE SUN'S CLOSEST NEIGHBOR. ALSO CALLED RIGEL KENTAURUS, IT IS LOCATED IN THE CONSTELLATION CENTAURUS, THE CENTAUR, ONE OF THE LARGEST CONSTELLATIONS.

Lupus

Microscopium

Corona Austrina

CENTAURUS

Telescopium

Ara

ALPHA CENTAURI   3

Crux

Pavo

Musca

Triangulum Australe

Apus

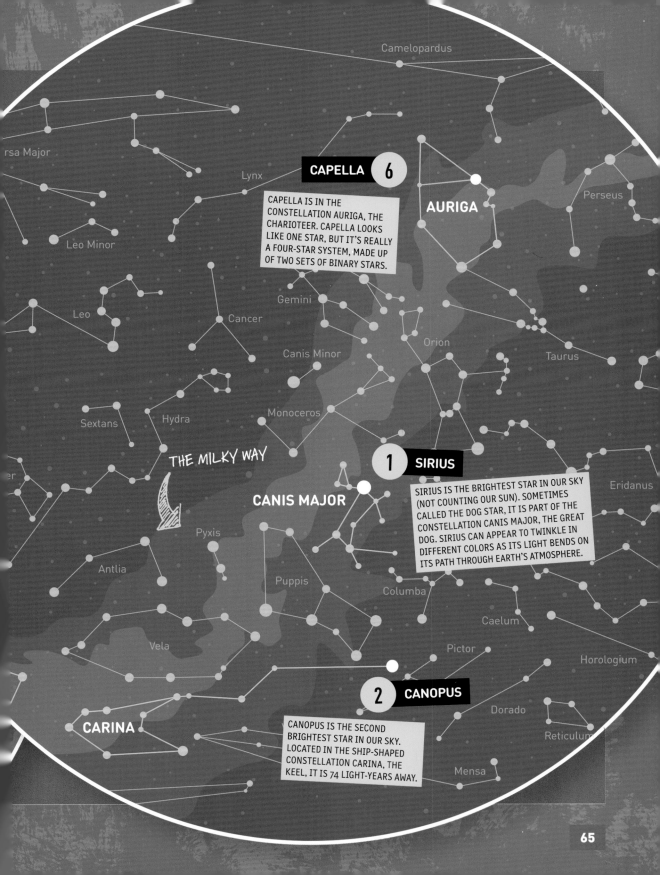

Camelopardus

Ursa Major

Lynx

CAPELLA **6**

CAPELLA IS IN THE CONSTELLATION AURIGA, THE CHARIOTEER. CAPELLA LOOKS LIKE ONE STAR, BUT IT'S REALLY A FOUR-STAR SYSTEM, MADE UP OF TWO SETS OF BINARY STARS.

AURIGA

Perseus

Leo Minor

Gemini

Leo

Cancer

Canis Minor

Orion

Taurus

Sextans

Hydra

Monoceros

THE MILKY WAY

1 **SIRIUS**

Eridanus

CANIS MAJOR

SIRIUS IS THE BRIGHTEST STAR IN OUR SKY (NOT COUNTING OUR SUN). SOMETIMES CALLED THE DOG STAR, IT IS PART OF THE CONSTELLATION CANIS MAJOR, THE GREAT DOG. SIRIUS CAN APPEAR TO TWINKLE IN DIFFERENT COLORS AS ITS LIGHT BENDS ON ITS PATH THROUGH EARTH'S ATMOSPHERE.

Pyxis

Antlia

Puppis

Columba

Caelum

Vela

Pictor

Horologium

2 **CANOPUS**

CARINA

Dorado

CANOPUS IS THE SECOND BRIGHTEST STAR IN OUR SKY. LOCATED IN THE SHIP-SHAPED CONSTELLATION CARINA, THE KEEL, IT IS 74 LIGHT-YEARS AWAY.

Reticulum

Mensa

SPACE LAB

MAKE A MODEL OF A BLACK HOLE

What's left over when a supernova explodes? A black hole. A black hole has superstrong gravity, so anything in space that gets near it is drawn into it. To understand more about black holes, grab a friend and these materials, and then follow the instructions on the next page.

What you need:

2 PEOPLE

HEAVY BALL (LIKE A BASEBALL OR A BILLIARD BALL)

MARBLES

STRETCHY FABRIC (LIKE A LYCRA SHIRT OR SPANDEX PANTS)

What to do:

HOW DOES THE MARBLE MOVE THROUGH "SPACE"?

1. **Each person picks up two corners of the fabric,** which represents two-dimensional space. The fabric should be held taut and still.

2. **Put the marble on top of the fabric.** Working together, tip the fabric to make the marble roll across the fabric. Observe how the marble moves through "space."

3. **Remove the marble and place the larger ball on the fabric.** Observe what happens to the fabric.

4. **Place the marble on the fabric again.** Tip the fabric to send the marble near the heavier ball. Observe the marble's behavior.

What's Happening

When the marble crosses "space" alone, it travels in a straight line. When the heavy ball crosses the fabric, the material sags. Space curves around it. When both the marble and heavier ball are on the fabric, the marble is unable to travel in a straight line. Instead, it begins to circle the heavier ball. Eventually, it falls next to it. In space, a black hole's gravity changes how other objects behave. The black hole deforms space in a way that brings light and other objects closer, preventing them from escaping.

WHAT HAPPENS WHEN THE MARBLE MOVES THROUGH "SPACE" WITH THE LARGER BALL?

CHAPTER 3

JOURNEY TO SPACE

AS AN ASTRONOMER, I STUDY THE UNIVERSE BY DOING RESEARCH.

Research is the process of asking questions and figuring out how to answer them. One of the most exciting things about research is that it's like working on a jigsaw puzzle.

MUNAZZA ALAM

If you have worked on a 500- or 1,000-piece puzzle, you may have looked at the box to help you figure out where to put the pieces. Doing research is like working on a puzzle with one twist: We don't have the box! We don't know what the big picture will look like. That's why researchers work together and share findings. It is impossible for one person to solve the puzzle alone.

My research focuses on studying the atmospheres of exoplanets. Understanding exoplanet atmospheres is an important research question for several reasons. First off, exoplanet atmospheres can help us understand how planets form and evolve over time.

We can learn about how planets *formed* by studying hot Jupiter atmospheres. That's because their atmospheres were acquired as the planets formed. So studying the atmospheric makeup of giant planets like hot Jupiters can tell us what the conditions were like as the planets were forming. We can learn about how planets *evolved* by studying the atmospheres of smaller planets like super-Earths. These planets were too small to hold on to an atmosphere as they formed, but they could have acquired one after they formed.

A planet's atmosphere also controls its present-day climate. Our neighbor Venus, for example, has thick clouds in its atmosphere that trap heat—leading to temperatures more than 800°F (427°C)!

Researchers ask questions that have not yet been answered. Sometimes, a research project's answer is later disproved with new results. Sometimes, we can make an important discovery accidentally. When doing research, it's important to remember that the way we understand the pieces of the puzzle and how they fit together may change over time. To do research, you have to be curious, ask questions, and keep looking up. You never know what you might find!

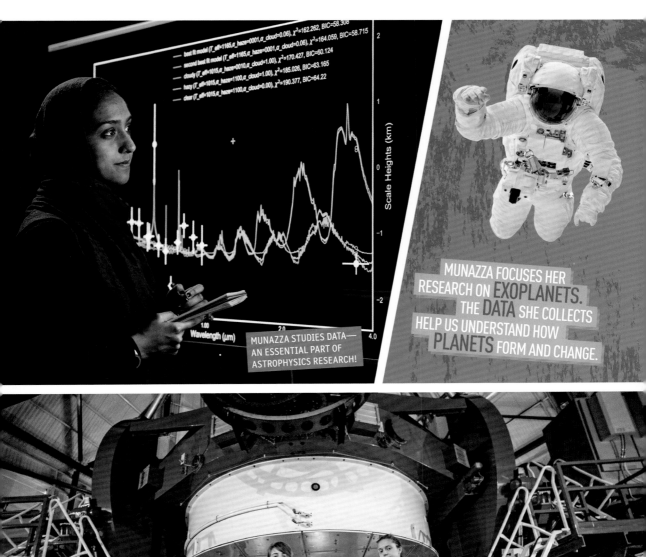

best fit model (T_{eff}=1165,σ_{haze}=0001,σ_{cloud}=0.06), χ^2=162.262, BIC=58.308
second best fit model (T_{eff}=1165,σ_{haze}=0001,σ_{cloud}=0.06), χ^2=164.059, BIC=58.715
cloudy (T_{eff}=1015,σ_{haze}=0010,σ_{cloud}=1.00), χ^2=170.427, BIC=60.124
hazy (T_{eff}=1015,σ_{haze}=1100,σ_{cloud}=1.00), χ^2=185.026, BIC=63.165
clear (T_{eff}=1015,σ_{haze}=1100,σ_{cloud}=0.00), χ^2=190.377, BIC=64.22

Scale Heights (km)

Wavelength (μm)

MUNAZZA STUDIES DATA— AN ESSENTIAL PART OF ASTROPHYSICS RESEARCH!

MUNAZZA FOCUSES HER RESEARCH ON EXOPLANETS. THE DATA SHE COLLECTS HELP US UNDERSTAND HOW PLANETS FORM AND CHANGE.

MUNAZZA (CENTER) STANDS WITH FELLOW RESEARCHERS HALEY FICA (LEFT) AND SARA CAMNASIO (RIGHT) IN FRONT OF THE MAGELLAN 1 BAADE TELESCOPE AT LAS CAMPANAS OBSERVATORY IN CHILE.

SATELLITES, ROBOTS, AND SPACECRAFT HELP UNLOCK THE SECRETS OF THE UNIVERSE.

Machines of the future will take us deeper into unknown worlds.

Why Explore Space?

When you visit a new place, you want to know more about it. You might think: How is it different from home? Can I find things I need here? Is it dangerous? People explore Earth and outer space for the same reasons. We are curious, we want to find things we can use, and we need to understand how our universe works. Knowing how objects move in space helps astronomers track asteroids and comets. We need to know how they behave—especially in case one gets close enough to strike Earth! Scientists study distant stars to understand our closest star, the sun, which affects life on Earth every single day. Learning about the universe and building technologies to explore space lead to new innovations that benefit people on Earth. When countries share what they learn about space, people from around the world come together through science.

Exploring From Earth

As of spring 2019, 236 people—from 18 countries—have spent time on the International Space Station since it launched. Visiting space is exciting, but it is also complicated and expensive. Luckily, thanks to the many ground telescopes pointed toward the sky, astronomers and other scientists can also explore space from right here on Earth.

Before the first telescopes, people falsely believed Earth was the center of the universe. Telescopes have forever changed our view. There are many different types of telescopes, and they have been used to discover new worlds, measure the speed of light, and understand the effects of gravity.

Optical telescopes are used to observe objects we can see with our eyes. They collect particles of light called photons and focus the visible light, making it stronger so that it can be analyzed. There are three types—reflectors, which use mirrors; refractors, which use lenses; and compound telescopes, which use both. A reflector's curved primary mirror collects light from the object being observed. Its smaller secondary mirror reflects the light to the eyepiece. Reflectors are good for observing objects that are farther away and fainter. Refractors, which use lenses, are like one side of a pair of binoculars. They are reliable, but not good for viewing distant galaxies and nebulae. It is easier to make a large mirror than a large lens, so the largest telescopes are reflectors. Compound telescopes offer benefits of both reflectors and refractors. They can be used in the day to see objects on Earth and at night to view faint objects in the sky. Astronomers mount instruments on telescopes that split light

OPTICAL TELESCOPES HELP US ZOOM IN ON OBJECTS WE CAN SEE WITH OUR EYES.

PARTS OF A RADIO TELESCOPE

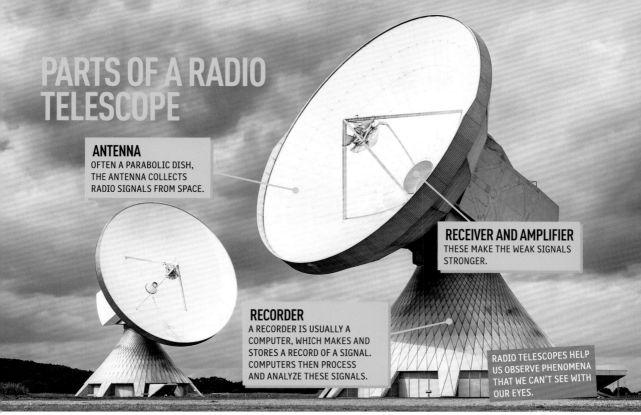

ANTENNA
OFTEN A PARABOLIC DISH, THE ANTENNA COLLECTS RADIO SIGNALS FROM SPACE.

RECEIVER AND AMPLIFIER
THESE MAKE THE WEAK SIGNALS STRONGER.

RECORDER
A RECORDER IS USUALLY A COMPUTER, WHICH MAKES AND STORES A RECORD OF A SIGNAL. COMPUTERS THEN PROCESS AND ANALYZE THESE SIGNALS.

RADIO TELESCOPES HELP US OBSERVE PHENOMENA THAT WE CAN'T SEE WITH OUR EYES.

into colors. This allows them to use their expertise to "read" the light and learn about the elements that make up different objects.

Radio telescopes, which look like giant satellite dishes, help us see what we can't with our eyes. They detect faint cosmic radio waves and let astronomers observe through clouds and dust to detect objects they otherwise couldn't. Radio waves that reach Earth from space are very weak—even cell phones transmit signals a billion times stronger—so radio telescopes are usually set in remote areas to avoid the interference of radio signals from Earth. Gamma rays, x-rays, ultraviolet light, and other types of electromagnetic radiation can also be detected with space-based telescopes.

THE DISH POINTS TO THE SKY IN AUSTRALIA.

The Dish

Nicknamed "the Dish," the Parkes Radio Telescope in Australia is one of the largest radio telescopes in the Southern Hemisphere. With a 210-foot (64-m) diameter, it is sensitive enough to find pulsars—and it finds lots of them. Originally built in 1961, but updated many times since, the Dish has located half of the more than 2,000 known pulsars. As well as peering into the universe, the Dish has been used to communicate with spacecraft and track their movements. When an explosion damaged part of the Apollo 13 spacecraft on its way to the moon in 1970, this telescope helped astronauts communicate with Mission Control in Houston, Texas, U.S.A. In 2012, it was used to help monitor NASA's Curiosity rover as it landed on Mars.

World's Largest Telescope Array

Radio waves may be as long as an American football or longer than Earth from pole to pole—these waves can be much longer than wavelengths from visible light. It is easier to study these giant waves by using a telescope array—a collection of telescopes spread out over a large area. The telescopes work together to act as one giant telescope. The Very Large Array (VLA) in New Mexico, U.S.A., includes 28 dishes. Each one is 82 feet (25 m) in diameter. The telescopes sit on a track, like a railway track, and can be tilted or spun into different positions for observing the sky.

Discoveries made using the VLA include ice on Mercury and a new type of object called a microquasar— an object like a quasar, but with a smaller black hole and an accretion disk that comes from a binary star system.

The Very Long Baseline Array (VLBA) is the world's largest array. Its 10 82-foot (25-m) dishes are placed across an area that covers 5,351 miles (8,612 km), stretching from Hawaii to the U.S. Virgin Islands. The VLBA has been used to map the magnetic field of a star, make movies that show motion inside supernova explosions, and study the hidden universe.

Exploring From Space

When you want a better look at something, you move closer to it. But when the object you want to see is in space, it's a lot more complicated! Even still, astronauts have walked on the moon. Satellites circle Earth, collecting and transmitting vast amounts of information. Robotic vehicles, or rovers, drive on Mars, and spacecraft with cameras tour the solar system. Two have even reached interstellar space—the region between the stars. Some astronauts temporarily live and work on space stations, and the technologies created to make space travel possible are used to improve life on Earth.

BUZZ ALDRIN, PHOTOGRAPHED BY FELLOW ASTRONAUT NEIL ARMSTRONG, STANDS ON THE SURFACE OF THE MOON.

THE VERY LARGE ARRAY IS A COLLECTION OF RADIO TELESCOPES IN NEW MEXICO, U.S.A.

THIS ARTWORK SHOWS THE VOYAGER SPACECRAFT EXPLORING PLACES HUMANS CAN'T GO—LIKE NEPTUNE.

THE VOYAGER SPACECRAFT

Let's take a look at some of the out-of-this-world ways that people explore space.

Spacecraft

For a closer look at space, you need a space-craft (also called a space probe) and a rocket powerful enough to escape Earth's gravity. The first spacecraft to escape Earth's gravity was the Soviet satellite Sputnik 1, which orbited Earth in 1957. Since that first historic moment, space exploration has changed the world.

A One-Way Trip

The first machines used to explore the solar system were flyby spacecraft. This type of spacecraft is designed to pass by a planet or other object in space without getting close enough to be pulled in by the object's gravity. Instruments on the spacecraft collect information and send it back to Earth. It takes a long time to plan a flyby. Aerospace engineers must start their work years before the launch date. They have to calculate the future location of the object they want the spacecraft to fly by, the speed needed to reach it, and the exact time to launch.

Flyby spacecraft are the simplest and cheapest way to visit objects in space, but they travel on a one-way ticket. After passing their targets, they are unable to return. The famous Voyager 2 is a flyby spacecraft used to examine Jupiter, Saturn, Uranus, Neptune, and the outermost regions of our solar system. Launched on August 20, 1977, Voyager 2 has been transmitting information about the solar system to Earth for more than 40 years. In 2018, it became the second spacecraft to travel beyond the solar system.

THE HUBBLE SPACE TELESCOPE DEPLOYS ONE OF ITS SOLAR ARRAY PANELS, WHICH PROVIDE IT WITH POWER.

A TELESCOPE IN SPACE

MOST TELESCOPES ARE FIRMLY SET ON THE GROUND, but the famous Hubble Space Telescope orbits Earth. Far above our atmosphere and light pollution (see Lights Out!, page 100), it has a clear view of the worlds beyond our planet. In fact, it can see faint, deep-space objects as far away as 13 billion light-years. That's all the way back to the early universe. Hubble circles the globe every 96 minutes, recording images and collecting information about deep space. A reflecting telescope, it has changed our understanding of the universe. Scientists have used it to help figure out the age of the universe and confirm that supermassive black holes exist at the center of galaxies. By combining information from ground-based telescopes, Hubble was used to create one image of 15,000 galaxies. It was launched into space on the space shuttle *Discovery* in 1990. Astronauts visit the telescope to install new instruments and do the maintenance needed to keep it working as it circles Earth from a height of 340 miles (547 km). It was named after Edwin Hubble (1889–1953), the American astronomer who first discovered other galaxies and that the universe is always expanding.

CASSINI LINES UP TO DIVE BETWEEN SATURN'S RINGS TO GATHER DATA BEFORE BURNING UP IN THE PLANET'S ATMOSPHERE.

Round and Round Again

Orbiter spacecraft are designed to enter the orbit of planets or other objects in space. They collect more in-depth information than a flyby spacecraft because they pass over the same areas of an object more than once. Orbiters allow scientists to see changes that occur on a planet over time. Within a few weeks or months, they can examine a planet's entire surface.

A SCIENTIFIC ILLUSTRATION SHOWS THE HUYGENS PROBE ENTERING TITAN'S UPPER ATMOSPHERE.

The Cassini-Huygens spacecraft, composed of the Cassini orbiter and the Huygens probe, traveled for nearly seven years before reaching Saturn in July 2004. The size and weight of a 30-passenger school bus, it was the largest and most costly probe to visit another planet. Cassini spent 13 years collecting information on Saturn, revealing amazing new science on the planet's rings, magnetic fields, and icy moons. Thanks to Cassini, scientists now know Saturn's moon—Titan—has many similarities to Earth, from clouds and rain to mountains and volcanoes.

In 2017, Cassini ran out of fuel. Scientists sent it hurtling through the gap between Saturn and its rings to gather information in a zone that had never before been observed. The spacecraft plunged through Saturn's atmosphere until pressure stopped its thrusters from working. Scientists knew the great mission was over when Cassini's antenna could no longer communicate with Earth.

Hop on Board

Sometimes spacecraft travel in pairs. Atmospheric spacecraft are probes that travel as passengers. They are not released until they are close enough to study the atmosphere of the planet they are visiting. Their instruments send data back to the partner spacecraft, which transmits it to Earth. The amazing Cassini-Huygens project involved two spacecraft traveling together to explore Saturn and Titan. Cassini carried Huygens, an atmospheric spacecraft fitted with instruments to analyze gases, measure light, and take other measurements. It also had the job of finding out whether Titan's surface was solid or covered with oceans.

Around 770 pounds (349 kg), Huygens was a large probe—about as heavy as two panda bears. In 2005, it descended below Titan's thick cloud layers, its two-hour trip ending on a floodplain littered with chunks of ice. It was the first spacecraft to land on a moon in the outer solar system. NASA, the European Space Agency, and the Italian Space Agency worked together to make this complicated mission possible.

It Takes a Team

Another way to explore a planet is to send spacecraft that can land on its surface, and these are sometimes sent in pairs. Landers carry instruments to collect information and transmit it to Earth. Some also transport wheeled spacecraft, called rovers, which take photos and use robotics to collect data from a small area on a planet's surface. Landers and rovers must be able to survive entry through a planet's atmosphere. The speed and angle must be just right to prevent the spacecraft from burning or breaking apart, and to make sure it lands in a safe spot. If the angle is too shallow, the spacecraft will continue its orbit. And since its path is elliptical, the spacecraft will return to reattempt a landing on the planet it is meant to explore. Unfortunately, the new angle of its approach is not likely to be any better, and the location of its entry may not allow it to reach a safe landing site.

After a spacecraft successfully passes through the atmosphere, it must reach the surface without becoming damaged on impact. It may use a parachute so it can descend slowly, as

ROVER
LANDER

THE MARS PATHFINDER SOJOURNER ROVER PREPARES TO EXPLORE THE SURFACE OF MARS.

well as a protective shell and air bags to cushion the landing. From Earth, scientists remotely steer the rover along the planet's surface. A rover's instruments might examine chemicals in rocks, look for water, and even search for signs of life.

During the last three Apollo missions (1971–72), astronauts explored the moon's terrain in electric lunar rovers. The longest trip in a moon buggy lasted four hours and 26 minutes and took the astronauts on a 22.3-mile (36-km) round trip. In 1997, NASA launched a lander— the Mars Pathfinder—to carry the first robotic rover to Mars. Protected by a collection of giant airbags, Pathfinder landed in a rocky floodplain.

Both the lander and the rover, called Sojourner, carried instruments that allowed scientists to analyze rocks and soil, and to learn about the atmosphere and weather on Mars.

Penetrator Spacecraft

Another type of probe does not just land, it also enters the surface of its landing site. A penetrator, or impactor, spacecraft may be sent to a planet, moon, comet, or other object. In 2005, NASA sent a spacecraft called Deep Impact 268 million miles (431 million km) to reach comet Tempel 1. This flyby spacecraft delivered an 820-pound (372-kg) impactor to the comet. It was the first mission to examine what lies below a comet's surface.

When the coffee-table-size impactor struck, it caused a huge cloud of fine powdery ice and dust to form. The mission revealed new information about comets. It found that the comet's deep interior was not affected by solar heat. This means it had probably not changed

NASA'S DEEP IMPACT PENETRATOR SNAPPED THIS IMAGE OF COMET TEMPEL 1 IN 2005—JUST WHEN THE COMET OBLITERATED THE SPACECRAFT.

THE SPITZER SPACE TELESCOPE CAN HELP US OBSERVE OBJECTS WE CAN'T SEE BY STUDYING THE BRIGHTNESS OF STARS WHEN DARK BODIES PASS BEFORE THEM.

AN EXAMPLE OF A SPACECRAFT BUS, THIS LUNAR ATMOSPHERE AND DUST ENVIRONMENT EXPLORER (LADEE) CARRIES ELECTRONICS AND PAYLOADS.

since the solar system first formed. The impactor also found evidence of water ice and organic compounds—the kinds of molecules that are found in life as we know it. Scientists think comets may have brought these compounds—the building blocks of life—to Earth. Using penetrator spacecraft to study comets—the oldest objects in the solar system—helps scientists better understand the origin of the universe.

Observatory Spacecraft

When you gaze into the night sky from Earth, you are looking through the layers of our planet's atmosphere. Warm and cool pockets of air around the planet rise and sink. This constant churning affects your view.

Most of what scientists learn about the universe comes from studying light, including light in the form of weak radio waves, only detectable with a radio telescope, or visible light from an optical telescope.

In space, light travels in a straight line. However, when it gets close to Earth, the light travels through moving pockets of air that act like lenses, making the light bend and bounce. This is why stars appear to twinkle.

Scientists get the best views of space by placing observatory spacecraft, like telescopes, in orbit outside Earth's atmosphere. In 2013, the powerful Spitzer Space Telescope was launched to study our solar system, as well as the most distant places in the universe. At 1,906 pounds (865 kg), Spitzer is twice the weight of a horse, and at 13 feet (4 m), it is about as long as a female giraffe is tall. An infrared observatory, Spitzer analyzes space radiation that cannot be studied from Earth because the atmosphere filters it out. Along with all the other great information it has collected, Spitzer was the first telescope to directly detect and study exoplanets.

WITH SPECIAL SENSORS, SATELLITES CAN PICK UP THE GLOW FROM NATURAL AND HUMAN-MADE LIGHT SOURCES AT NIGHT.

NASA'S SUOMI NPP SATELLITE CAPTURED THIS IMAGE OF THE UNITED STATES AT NIGHT IN 2012. SATELLITES CAN TAKE PICTURES AND COLLECT SCIENTIFIC DATA ABOUT EARTH AND OTHER OBJECTS IN SPACE.

Catching a Bus to Space

You can't hop on a space bus like you can a school bus. Spacecraft buses are platforms that house equipment needed for a space mission, from batteries and computers to antennas and thrusters. Just as a tripod holds a telescope, a spacecraft bus provides a place to attach equipment. Spacecraft buses also hold payloads—everything that is not part of the structure, including satellites, telescopes, and other research equipment. An octagonal spacecraft bus supports the Spitzer Space Telescope. Its bays hold the solar panels that power the telescope's instruments and the gyroscopes that allow astronomers to point the telescope. The bus, also called a service module, contains everything needed to control the telescope, communicate with Earth, and transmit the scientific data it collects.

I Spy From Way Up High

Launched into space with rockets, artificial satellites are engineered machines that orbit planets or other objects in space and collect or transmit data. Satellites can be used to take pictures and collect scientific information about Earth and other objects in space. They allow scientists to track storms and predict weather, monitor ozone and other gases in the atmosphere, and measure cosmic rays. Satellites can also be used for military purposes, such as to watch nuclear sites. Using radio, television, or telephone signals, communication satellites transmit information around the world. More than 20 communications satellites make up the Global Positioning System (GPS), transmitting data that allow users to know their exact location.

While GPS satellites orbit Earth twice a day, other satellites can loop Earth in 90 minutes, transferring their data 16 times a day. Artificial satellites orbiting Earth may follow a polar route—a north-south path that loops from pole to pole. Others follow a geostationary path, moving from west to east over the Equator. Geostationary satellites travel at the same speed Earth is spinning. This makes them appear locked in one place, over one spot on Earth.

Satellites may travel from a few hundred to thousands of miles overhead. Using radio signals, they transmit the information they collect down to Earth. Ground stations receive the signals they send.

SPACEPLANES!

AFTER A ROCKET'S STAGES SEPARATE from the main body, they either burn up in Earth's atmosphere or fall into an ocean, where they litter the ocean floor. To avoid this waste, NASA began to explore reusable rockets. In 1981, it launched its first space shuttle, a spacecraft designed to shoot into the sky like a rocket but land on a runway like a glider airplane. The shuttles replaced expensive one-time-use rockets and enabled human spaceflight in low Earth orbit—the first 100 to 200 miles (161 to 322 km) of space. With room for up to seven astronauts, space shuttles were used to conduct laboratory research, deliver and

THE SPACE SHUTTLE *ATLANTIS* LANDS AT CAPE CANAVERAL, FLORIDA, U.S.A., IN 2011.

retrieve satellites, and repair orbiting spacecraft, like the Hubble Space Telescope. Later missions helped build the International Space Station. The fleet flew 135 missions over a 30-year period that ended in 2011.

Some satellites are part of a fleet. The fleet operated by the U.S. National Oceanic and Atmospheric Administration (NOAA) is called the Joint Polar Satellite System. So far, two of its five satellites have been launched, and an instrument contributing data to the fleet has been placed on a U.S. Air Force Space Test Program satellite. The satellites cross Earth's Equator about 14 times each day as they travel around the planet in a polar orbit. They provide most of the information used to make U.S. weather forecasts and provide important data during blizzards, hurricanes, tornadoes, and other severe weather events. The fleet can also detect droughts, forest fires, poor air quality, and other dangerous conditions. All the fleet's satellites will have been launched by 2031.

THE SOYUZ TMA-05M ROCKET BLASTS OFF FROM THE BAIKONUR COSMODROME IN KAZAKHSTAN IN 2012.

Blast Off!

Rockets are powerful machines that can be used to transport spacecraft and their payloads, including astronauts, into space. Unlike jet engines, which need air to work, rocket engines can operate in space. Newton's third law—every action has an equal and opposite reaction—explains how rockets work: When rocket fuel is heated, it expands and shoots out the bottom of the rocket. This creates an opposite reaction—pushing the rocket up. However, rockets need a lot of fuel to escape Earth's gravity. Their fuel is stored in different compartments, called stages. When the fuel in one stage is used up, the stage separates from the main rocket. Now lighter, the rocket goes even faster. It must reach a speed of nearly 25,000 miles an hour (40,234 km/h) to escape Earth and enter into orbit.

The most powerful type of rocket is called a heavy lift launch vehicle. The giant Saturn V is the mightiest rocket ever built. Taller than the Statue of Liberty, it was used to send astronauts to the moon and launch the first U.S. space station.

Smaller rockets, called sounding rockets, are used to carry scientific instruments into space on short trips that may only last from five to 20 minutes. They travel at lower speeds than other rockets and can collect data in areas too low for satellites.

The International Space Station

Imagine a research station in space, where astronauts live and conduct experiments, and you will be picturing the International Space Station (ISS). Traveling five miles a second (8 km/s) the station orbits Earth about 25 times faster than the speed of sound! The ISS looks like a long tube. Tunnels connect its different parts, called modules, and the entire station is as big as an American football field. The area where astronauts live is about the size of a five-bedroom house. Giant solar panels collect energy from the sun to power the station and create oxygen for astronauts to breathe. Crews have been living on the ISS since 2000. It takes three astronauts to run the station, but 10 might be on board at one time, running experiments and working to keep the station operating properly. Most missions last around six months.

EXPERTS AROUND THE GLOBE

AN INTERNATIONAL CREW POSES FOR A PHOTO ON THE ISS.

IT TOOK EXPERTS FROM MANY DIFFERENT COUNTRIES to build the International Space Station. The U.S. and Russia put it together in space, and other countries helped by building parts and sharing information. Fifteen countries work together to keep the space station running. The ISS partners are the U.S., Russia, Canada, Japan, and the European Space Agency, which includes 22 European countries: Austria, Belgium, Czech Republic, Denmark, Estonia, Finland, France, Germany, Greece, Hungary, Ireland, Italy, Luxembourg, the Netherlands, Norway, Poland, Portugal, Romania, Spain, Sweden, Switzerland, and the United Kingdom.

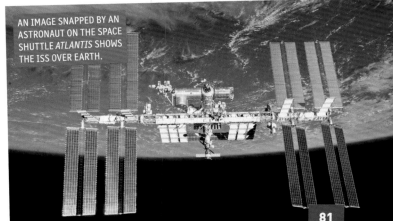

AN IMAGE SNAPPED BY AN ASTRONAUT ON THE SPACE SHUTTLE *ATLANTIS* SHOWS THE ISS OVER EARTH.

EARLY SPACE STATIONS

THE U.S.'S FIRST SPACE STATION, SKYLAB, ORBITED EARTH FOR SIX YEARS. THREE DIFFERENT CREWS OF ASTRONAUTS CIRCLED EARTH, MAKING A TOTAL OF 2,476 ORBITS FROM 1973 TO 1979. MISSION WORK INCLUDED SOLAR OBSERVATIONS AND NEARLY 300 EXPERIMENTS. SKYLAB PROVED HUMANS COULD LIVE IN SPACE FOR LONG PERIODS—ONE MISSION SPENT 84 DAYS IN SPACE.

SKYLAB

BUILT FROM 1986 TO 1996, THE RUSSIAN SPACE STATION MIR SPENT 15 YEARS IN ORBIT. HOME TO 23,000 EXPERIMENTS, IT ACHIEVED MANY FIRSTS. IT WAS THE FIRST SPACE STATION TO BE ASSEMBLED IN ORBIT, IT HOUSED THE FIRST CROP OF WHEAT GROWN FROM SEED TO SEED IN SPACE, AND IT WAS INVOLVED IN THE DEVELOPMENT OF THE SHUTTLE-MIR PROGRAM, WHICH SAW THE U.S. AND RUSSIA WORK TOGETHER TO ADVANCE SPACE EXPLORATION.

MIR

TIANGONG-1

THE CHINA NATIONAL SPACE ADMINISTRATION BUILT A SPACE STATION CALLED TIANGONG-1, WHICH MEANS "HEAVENLY PALACE—ONE." THE STATION WAS BUILT TO TEST THE ROBOTIC TECHNOLOGIES CHINA WILL NEED TO BUILD A MORE ELABORATE SPACE STATION IN THE EARLY 2020s. TIANGONG-1 ORBITED EARTH FROM 2011 TO 2018. TWO CREWS OF ASTRONAUTS, CALLED TAIKONAUTS, VISITED THE STATION FOR SHORT MISSIONS LASTING AROUND TWO WEEKS EACH.

THE ABC's OF SPACE AGENCIES

NASA, ESA, CSA ... We use lots of letters when we talk about space. Most countries' space programs go by acronyms—names formed just from the first letter of each word in their name. Here's a list so you can keep them straight:

COUNTRY	SPACE PROGRAM	ACRONYM	LOCATION
UNITED STATES	National Aeronautics and Space Administration	NASA	Washington, D.C.
CANADA	Canadian Space Agency	CSA	Saint-Hubert, Quebec
EUROPE	European Space Agency	ESA	Paris, France
JAPAN	Japan Aerospace Exploration Agency	JAXA	Tokyo
CHINA	China National Space Administration	CNSA	Beijing
INDIA	Indian Space Research Organization	ISRO	Bangalore
RUSSIA	State Space Corporation	ROSCOSMOS	Moscow

Space Litter

What happens to a broken-down spacecraft that no longer works or serves any purpose? Some of it orbits Earth. Other pieces float in space. Out-of-use spacecraft, as well as anything left in space by humans, is called space junk, and it may be as small as a chip of paint or as big as a truck. It includes rocket boosters, a glove lost on a space walk, broken satellites, and bits of debris formed when human-made objects collide in space. Because space junk orbits Earth at 17,500 miles an hour (28,164 km/h), even a paint chip can damage a spacecraft. Scientists track more than half a million pieces of space junk larger than a softball as they orbit Earth. They can warn the International Space Station if a collision might happen, and the ISS can move out of the way. However, millions of pieces are too small to track. Over time, gravity pulls pieces orbiting within 373 miles (600 km) of Earth into the atmosphere. As the space trash passes through the air, friction creates intense heat and most of it burns up.

Space junk is expensive to remove. Although no international laws are in place to force cleanup, space organizations are working on ways to reduce the litter they create and ways to remove the space debris already out there. Solutions might involve the use of lasers, nets, or giant harpoons.

REAL DATA FROM NASA'S ORBITAL DEBRIS PROGRAM OFFICE SHOW SPACE LITTER ORBITING EARTH.

READY, SET, GO— TO SPACE!

ASTRONAUT ALAN SHEPARD, JR., IS PICKED UP BY A HELICOPTER SHORTLY AFTER RETURNING TO EARTH. HE WAS THE FIRST AMERICAN EVER IN SPACE.

THE RACE TO SPACE BEGAN AFTER WORLD WAR II, when the United States and the U.S.S.R. (Union of Soviet Socialist Republics, a supergroup of republics whose area today includes Russia, Lithuania, Ukraine, and more) became the world's two superpowers. The two rivals tried to stop each other from becoming more powerful, and a new era began. It was called the Cold War because neither country directly attacked the other. Both the U.S. and the U.S.S.R. wanted to prove superiority and stop the other from having a military advantage—not just on Earth but in space, too.

The Space Race began in the late 1950s. When the U.S.S.R. launched the world's first satellite, Sputnik, the U.S. formed NASA. The U.S.'s goal was to put people on the moon before the U.S.S.R. could. Russian cosmonaut Yuri Gagarin was the first person to orbit Earth. On April 12, 1961, he orbited Earth for 108 minutes and returned safely. Less than a month later, U.S. astronaut Alan Shepard became the first American in space.

His 15-minute flight on May 5, 1961, was not as long as Gagarin's, but it was still impressive and it did show that the Americans were still in the race.

The Space Race continued, with each country achieving different firsts. The Soviet space program sent the first probe—Luna 2—to the moon in 1959, but in 1968, the U.S. sent the first astronauts to orbit the moon in Apollo 8. In 1969, the Apollo 11 mission put a lander carrying astronauts on the moon, and American Neil Armstrong become the first man to walk on its surface, followed by his fellow astronaut Buzz Aldrin. With this remarkable feat, the U.S. won the Space Race.

In 1975, a new era of cooperation began. The U.S. and the U.S.S.R. planned the Apollo-Soyuz Test Project, a meeting in space to test the rendezvous system—designed to bring two spacecraft in close orbits together—and the docking system needed to connect two spacecraft in space. When Apollo docked with the Soviet spacecraft Soyuz, three U.S. astronauts and two Soviet cosmonauts exchanged flags in space. They also conducted five experiments. Today, U.S. and Russian cooperation continues on the International Space Station.

A SOVIET TECHNICIAN WORKS ON SPUTNIK, THE WORLD'S FIRST SATELLITE, IN 1957.

Space Technology Spin-Offs

In order for humans and machinery to live and work in the harsh environment of space, engineers and scientists must invent new technologies. Many of these inventions can be adapted to solve problems or make life easier on Earth. For example, NASA had to figure out a way to provide astronauts with drinking water in space. Water on the ISS is made using a system that reclaims and purifies water found in sweat, urine, and exhaled breaths, as well as wastewater from washing, toothbrushing, and shaving. The technologies it created are now adapted to provide clean water during natural disasters and help communities that do not have access to clean water. Technologies first developed for astronomy or space exploration are called technology transfer, or simply "spin-offs."

Donning a Suit for Space

Astronauts preparing to work outside the ISS must first step into a special kind of spacecraft designed to create an artificial Earth-like environment—in a suit! It's commonly called a space suit, but NASA's official name is Extravehicular Mobility Unit, or EMU for short. The suit is all that exists between the astronaut and the dangers of space—radiation, no oxygen to breathe, and a lack of air pressure. On Earth, air pressure keeps the fluids in a person's body in a liquid state. Without air pressure, a person's body fluids will boil. The EMU is made of interlocking pieces that allow the astronaut to move, while making sure no skin is ever exposed to space. Temperatures outside the station are extreme. It can be as hot as 250°F (121°C) and as cold as minus 250°F (-157°C). The space suit's layers of tough material protect the astronaut from temperature extremes, as well as from micrometeoroids. These small particles of space dust can puncture a suit and cause injury because they travel at very high speeds—up to five miles a second (8 km/s).

Under the suit, the astronaut wears a "Snoopy cap" that contains a microphone and headphones for communication. They also wear a liquid-cooling garment. Covering the full body, it contains tubes of cool water that help keep the astronaut at a comfortable body temperature. A display and control module on the astronaut's chest includes switches to control the radio, oxygen, cooling system, and other processes. Switch labels are written in reverse so the astronaut can read them with a mirror mounted on the wrist of the suit. A visor assembly—fitted on the helmet—includes cameras, spotlights, and a visor for protection from the bright sun. An EMU makes it possible for an astronaut to work outside the ISS for up to eight hours.

A Day on the ISS

Living in space is literally out of this world—but it also involves work. Astronauts on the International Space Station have a busy schedule that always involves thinking about safety. They monitor the space station's many different systems and keep up with repairs and maintenance. Astronauts also have to do chores.

DURING DOWNTIME ON THE ISS, NASA ASTRONAUT DAN BURBANK STRUMS THE GUITAR WHILE RUSSIAN COSMONAUT ANTON SHKAPLEROV PLAYS THE KEYBOARD.

They unload cargo shipments, vacuum air vents, and disinfect surfaces to control bacteria. They even hand-crush garbage so it takes up less space before being shipped out in a supply vehicle.

The ISS is a giant laboratory in space, so astronauts also have research to do. They run science experiments that can only be done in weak gravity, also known as microgravity, where objects are almost weightless and float around. For example, on Earth, a liquid must be held in a container, otherwise gravity will spill it toward the ground. A spilled liquid on the ISS, however, will respond to microgravity by floating in a spherical shape. Microgravity allows astronauts to study a liquid's characteristics and experiment with chemical reactions without interference or contamination from a container. Astronauts take part in medical experiments, too, to learn how the human body reacts to living in space for long periods. To do their work, astronauts must communicate with mission control centers and coordinate their schedules to match different time zones on Earth.

Astronauts also need time to take care of personal needs, like eating, keeping clean, and exercising. A space workout means spending two and a half hours on exercise equipment every day! Because of the weightless environment, astronauts must exercise daily to keep their muscles strong.

Living in space isn't all work, though. Astronauts have free time in their schedules and get weekends off, too. They might spend time reading, watching movies, playing or listening to music, taking photos, playing cards, or keeping in touch with family through email and video chats. One favorite pastime is looking outside. Sunrises and sunsets occur every 45 minutes as the station orbits Earth. Astronauts say they are fascinated and awed by the view of Planet Earth from space.

HOW CAN YOU BECOME AN ASTRONAUT?

GET INVOLVED IN ACTIVITIES THAT TEACH leadership, communication, and teamwork. You'll be living in a spacecraft without a lot of room, so it helps to know how to get along with other people.

STUDY HARD! Astronauts focus on complex subjects like engineering, medicine, math, or a science. They usually get a college degree in one of these fields because they need to learn how to solve problems like an engineer and conduct research as a scientist.

BECOME A PILOT. Many astronauts have been military pilots. In addition to teaching other skills, like an understanding of aerodynamics, flight training builds quick decision-making skills that can be important in space.

WORK FOR AT LEAST THREE YEARS IN YOUR FIELD. Whether that's flying, science, medicine, or something else, it's helpful to have experience on Earth before you go to space.

BE ABLE TO SPEAK ENGLISH AND RUSSIAN. Astronauts on the ISS must know some Russian. It's important to be able to talk with everyone on your mission.

WORK AT KEEPING FIT AND HEALTHY. Astronauts need to be in good physical shape to have the stamina needed for space walks, and to handle emergencies that could occur in space or when returning to Earth.

GET STARTED NOW! Read books that explore science, engineering, and space and visit the websites of space agencies around the world.

"Hey— you've already started! See you in space!"

SPACE WATCH: SPOT A SATELLITE OR SPACE JUNK!

Satellites in the night sky become visible when sunlight reflects off their surfaces, often as sunlight strikes a satellite's solar panels. Even though the sun has disappeared over Earth's horizon, it has not set for the satellites orbiting 200 to 300 miles (322 to 483 km) overhead. The best time to see satellites is dusk and dawn. Most of the time, you will probably spot one within 15 minutes of watching.

When you see what looks like a star slowly crossing the sky, you have spotted a satellite. You will be able to track it for several minutes, sometimes longer. The brightness remains steady for most satellites, though sometimes a flash occurs when sunlight strikes a reflective surface at just the right angle. Satellites always follow a straight line and travel at a consistent speed, disappearing from sight when they enter Earth's shadow.

Sometimes the light you see crossing the sky is sunlight reflecting off space junk orbiting Earth. Space junk and satellites may blink in a rhythmic pattern due to a tumbling motion. They will be much dimmer than the flashing lights of an airplane.

NASA's apps can show you how to find its Earth-orbiting satellites and the ISS. You can browse these apps by visiting this website: *nasa.gov/connect/apps.html*.

Get an adult's help when doing research online!

AIRPLANE

- Flashing lights
- May travel in a curved path or make a turn
- Speed may change

A LONG-EXPOSURE IMAGE SHOWS THE INTERNATIONAL SPACE STATION AS IT PASSES OVERHEAD.

AIRPLANE OR SATELLITE?

SATELLITE

- No flashing lights
- Brightness usually stays the same
- Travels in a straight line
- Speed does not change

A LONG-EXPOSURE PHOTO SHOWS AIRPLANE LINES ALONGSIDE STARS IN THE NIGHT SKY.

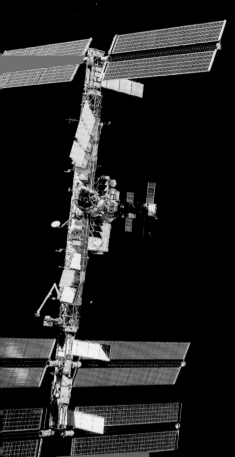

WHEN YOU SPOT THE INTERNATIONAL SPACE STATION, you will be seeing the largest and brightest human-made object orbiting Earth. It becomes visible at times near dusk or dawn, when sunlight reflects off its surface. You cannot see it in the middle of the night because it is in Earth's shadow, unable to reflect sunlight.

The station's highly reflective solar panels can make it appear as bright as Venus. Visible in different locations from night to night, the ISS may sometimes cross your view of the sky several times a week, monthly, or less often. At times, you may be able to see it multiple times in one morning or evening because it orbits Earth every 90 minutes.

The best way to find out when the ISS will travel over your area at a dark time is to visit the NASA website *(spotthestation .nasa.gov)* and enter your location into the map. The station will appear and disappear at the exact moment the site indicates, always at least 40 degrees over the westerly horizon, traveling east. It is important to be facing the right direction and watching closely. Sometimes it appears and disappears quite suddenly as it enters or leaves Earth's shadow. Since the ISS is traveling so fast, it will come and go in just a few minutes.

THE SPACE SHUTTLE *DISCOVERY* DOCKS ON THE INTERNATIONAL SPACE STATION.

THE HUBBLE SPACE TELESCOPE, ORBITING HERE AT 353 MILES (568 KM) OVER EARTH

THE HUBBLE TELESCOPE is best seen at latitudes between 28.5° north and 28.5° south. This includes places south of Orlando, Florida, U.S.A., and north of La Viña, Catamarca, Argentina. To spot it, you need to check the internet for locations and dates when it will be visible. In the search field, enter your location and the words "see Hubble telescope."

SPACE LAB

MAKE A ROCKET!

Ready to blast off? Experiment with rocket thrust and gravity with this experiment. Only in this activity, *you're* the rocket booster! Gather the materials on the opposite page, and then follow the instructions below!

ASK AN ADULT IF YOU NEED HELP!

What to do:

1. **On one piece of paper,** draw a rocket (or trace the template on the opposite page) and cut out the shape.

2. **Roll the remaining piece of paper around your straw.** You want it to be tight enough for a close fit, but loose enough for the straw to easily fit inside. Tape the paper to secure the roll.

3. **Measure the rolled-up paper to fit the rocket's length,** and tape one end tightly closed so that no air can pass through.

4. **Tape the rolled-up paper to your rocket,** lining up the closed end with the rocket's nose.

BLAST OFF!

5. **Slip the rolled-up paper over the straw,** and blow through the straw to launch the rocket.

6. **Experiment. Make more rockets using heavier paper, then cardboard.** Point the straw at different angles and see how far each rocket travels. Try adding cardboard fins or paper clips for weight and watch what happens. Try blowing really hard and then really softly. How far can you make a straw rocket fly?

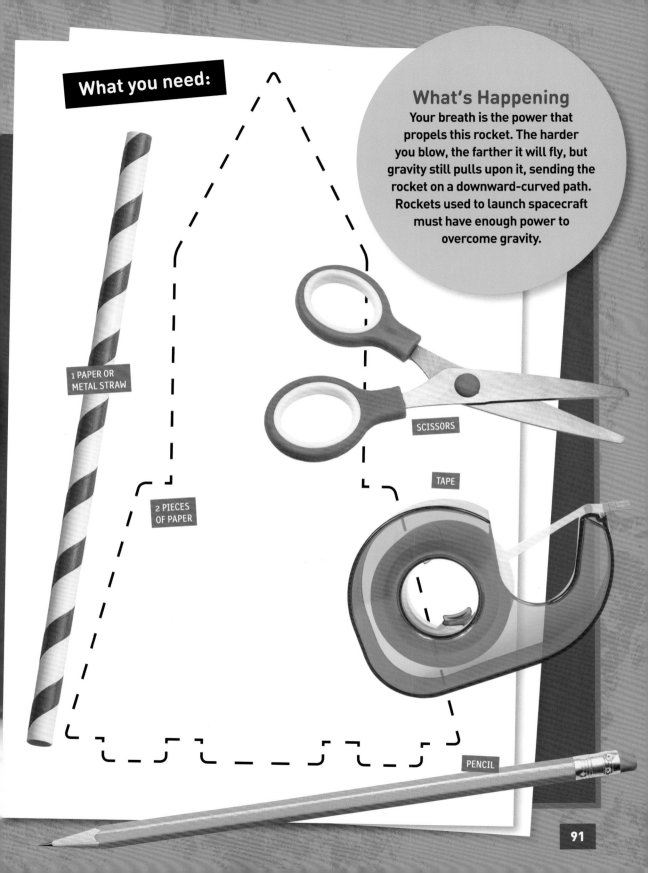

What you need:

1 PAPER OR METAL STRAW

2 PIECES OF PAPER

SCISSORS

TAPE

PENCIL

What's Happening

Your breath is the power that propels this rocket. The harder you blow, the farther it will fly, but gravity still pulls upon it, sending the rocket on a downward-curved path. Rockets used to launch spacecraft must have enough power to overcome gravity.

IN THIS IMAGE OF THE BARRED SPIRAL GALAXY NGC 1672, CLUSTERS OF YOUNG STARS SHINE LIGHT BLUE IN THE GALAXY'S SPIRAL ARMS.

CHAPTER 4

OUR
UNIVERSE

INTRODUCTION

CURRENTLY, PLANET EARTH IS THE ONLY PLACE WE KNOW OF THAT HOSTS LIFE.

But humans have wondered if life exists elsewhere in the universe since the beginning of time. This age-old question—"Are we alone?"—is one that my research seeks to answer.

MUNAZZA ALAM

Understanding the atmospheres of exoplanets can help us figure out if the conditions on these planets would be suitable for life.

My dream is to find an "Earth twin" exoplanet. This kind of planet would have liquid water, like oceans and lakes, on its surface. So we are looking for planets that are in the habitable zone, a Goldilocks region that is just right for hosting a planet with liquid water. If the planet is too close to its star, it will be too hot and the water will boil and evaporate from the planet's surface. If the planet is too far from its star, it will be too cold to have oceans, and any water that is on the planet will freeze into ice.

In our solar system, Earth lies in this Goldilocks region and is the only planet in our solar neighborhood that has liquid water! Our neighbor Venus, which is closer to the sun, is extremely hot and doesn't have any water on its surface. Our other neighbor Mars is farther away from the sun, and all of its surface water is frozen.

We might be able to find planets that host life by searching for biosignatures, or the fingerprints of life, in the atmospheres of these planets. Some of these biosignatures include oxygen, ozone, water, and carbon dioxide. These are molecules that are in the atmosphere of Earth as a result of the life-forms that exist on our home planet.

We currently do not have the telescope facilities capable of detecting the molecules that might help us determine if we have found a habitable planet. We need bigger telescopes that can observe at the wavelengths, or colors, of light where we would expect to see a signature of these molecules. In the future, astronomers hope to use Extremely Large Telescopes (ELTs) and the James Webb Space Telescope to detect these biosignatures.

IN THIS ILLUSTRATION, THE JAMES WEBB SPACE TELESCOPE RAISES A SHIELD AGAINST THE SUN TO PROTECT ITS MECHANICS.

WITH THE DEVELOPMENT OF MORE POWERFUL TELESCOPES, RESEARCHERS MIGHT ONE DAY BE ABLE TO DETECT BIOSIGNATURES, OR SIGNS OF LIFE, IN SPACE.

KEPLER-186F, PICTURED IN THIS ILLUSTRATION, IS THE FIRST EARTH-SIZE PLANET FOUND IN THE HABITABLE ZONE OF A STAR. IT'S ABOUT 500 LIGHT-YEARS FROM EARTH.

COULD THERE BE LIFE HERE?

EVERYTHING STARTED WITH A BANG ABOUT 13.8 BILLION YEARS AGO.

That's when the universe began. Before it existed, space, matter, and even time did not exist.

The Big Bang

Everything in the universe is moving apart. That means everything in the universe must have been closer together at one time. The most widely accepted explanation for the universe's motion and how it came to be is called the big bang. According to this theory, nearly 14 billion years ago, the entire observable universe contained only radiation and very small hot particles of matter compressed in a tiny dense point, called a singularity. This point was thousands of times smaller than the head on a pin and existed for less than a second.

The big bang was the beginning of the universe's expansion. The dense point began to spread outward. In under a second, it grew to the size of a galaxy and continued to expand at a rapid rate. Over great lengths of time, its particles joined together to form atoms, and the atoms joined together, eventually forming stars and galaxies. Even now, billions of years later, the universe continues to expand.

Clusters of Galaxies

Most galaxies exist in groups connected by gravity. A group may contain two galaxies orbiting one another, or thousands of galaxies in a cluster. The galaxies, along with great clouds of hot gas between them, orbit around a common point.

The Milky Way is part of a cluster called the Local Group. Its more than 50 members include the massive and bright Andromeda galaxy, a spiral galaxy like the Milky Way. Most of the others are low-mass dwarf galaxies. Small and dim, they are the most common type of galaxies in the universe.

Local Group galaxies stretch across a space that fills 10 million light-years. Even though the expanding universe pushes galaxies outward, gravity can cause close-together galaxies to collide. In a few billion years, the Milky Way and the Andromeda galaxies will merge together.

AN ILLUSTRATION SHOWS WHAT THE BIG BANG MIGHT HAVE LOOKED LIKE.

AN ARTIST'S ILLUSTRATION SHOWS CLUSTERS OF NEARBY GALAXIES. OUR GALAXY, THE MILKY WAY, IS IN THE LOCAL GROUP.

THE LOCAL GROUP

INVISIBLE PARTICLES

HOLD YOUR HAND UP IN THE SUNLIGHT and about a billion neutrinos will pass through it in just one second. Neutrinos out-number any other particle in the universe. They travel nearly as fast as the speed of light, passing through planets, stars, and galaxies. Neutrinos are tiny particles with nearly no mass and no electrical charge. They earned the nickname "ghost particles" because without an electrical charge, neutrinos barely interact with other types of matter. That makes them hard to find.

Scientists study neutrinos at the South Pole Neutrino Observatory in Antarctica. It operates a neutrino detector called IceCube, made up of a cubic kilometer (.23 cubic mile) of Antarctic ice that extends downward 8,200 feet (2,500 m). The very clear Antarctic ice is ideal for detecting neutrinos. As the weak particles travel through the ice, they interact with it and create other particles. This allows scientists to determine the neutrinos' direction and energy. Studying ghost particles can help scientists explore how matter evolves into more complex structures and better understand how the universe evolved.

THE WORLD'S LARGEST NEUTRINO OBSERVATORY, THE ICECUBE DETECTOR, IS LOCATED IN ANTARCTICA.

Dark Matter and Dark Energy

Most of the gravity holding galaxy clusters together comes from something invisible and mysterious called dark matter. Scientific instruments cannot see dark matter. It does not emit light, absorb light, or even reflect light. However, scientists can detect dark matter by observing how its gravity affects light. Dark matter makes up 27 percent of the universe.

Scientists believe dark matter exists because the gravity from ordinary matter, which is made up of atoms, is not strong enough to explain the motion in galaxies and galaxy clusters. Ordinary matter includes everything we can see. It makes up only 5 percent of the universe and is referred to as the visible universe. Galaxies and galaxy clusters rotate at such high speeds, they would be torn apart if only ordinary matter were present.

That leaves 68 percent for another mysterious component—dark energy! For a long time, it was believed that gravity must slow the universe's expansion, but observations made with the Hubble Space Telescope changed that. Scientists named dark energy following the 1998 observation of a supernova, which showed the expansion of the universe is speeding up. Before this time, scientists expected the expansion rate was either slowing down or remaining constant. They suggested that a force called dark energy was responsible. Scientists are still developing theories to understand dark energy.

USING DIFFERENT LAYERS OF PHOTOS AND DATA, NASA CAN CREATE AN IMAGE OF DARK MATTER, GALAXIES, AND HOT GAS IN THE CLUSTER ABELL 520.

THE MAGNETOSPHERE WEATHERS A BLAST OF SOLAR PARTICLES.

WHEN SOLAR FLARES (LEFT) SEND PARTICLES SHOOTING TOWARD EARTH, OUR MAGNETOSPHERE CAN BE AFFECTED.

INVISIBLE DANGER

RADIATION IS A TYPE OF ENERGY that travels as rays, waves, and particles. It can damage or kill human cells, but like a protective bubble, Earth's magnetic field and atmosphere shield us from most radiation. Space radiation, which is more dangerous than radiation on Earth, exists in three forms: as solar particles, galactic cosmic rays, and particles trapped in Earth's magnetic field.

SOLAR PARTICLES occur when flares on the sun send high-energy charged particles speeding through space. Traveling at 62,137 miles a second (100,000 km/s) solar particles can be powerful enough to damage satellites and interfere with radio communication. They can also be a health hazard for crews in high-flying aircraft.

GALACTIC COSMIC RAYS (GCRs) are a type of space radiation that originates outside the solar system. Most come from supernovae, and they can travel close to the speed of light. GCRs form inside the gas and magnetic field of a supernova remnant, which can exist for thousands of years. Bouncing back and forth inside the remnant, some of the particles gain energy and speed. Once powerful enough, the galactic cosmic rays escape the supernova remnant.

Closer to Earth, **SPACE RADIATION** trapped in the Van Allen belts sometimes escapes, entering space or Earth's atmosphere. The radiation, which can damage satellites, can also be harmful to astronauts. They wear detectors to keep track of how much radiation enters their bodies. In low Earth orbit, the planet's atmosphere and magnetic field still provide some protection; however, those visiting the moon or Mars will face more risk.

Hello Out There

With such a vast universe, it is hard to believe Earth is the only place where life exists. Astrobiologists and exobiologists are scientists interested in the search for life in space. One of the steps to finding life beyond our planet is to locate an exoplanet or moon with an environment where life could survive. To support the kind of life that exists on our planet, the planet must be Earth-like. That means it must have a similar size and mass, have liquid water on its surface, and be in the habitable zone, also called the Goldilocks zone. This is where the planet or moon is at a distance from its star where liquid water could exist on its surface. The temperature must be neither too hot or too cold, just like the porridge in the fairy tale "Goldilocks and the Three Bears."

Another step to understanding what life might look like on another planet involves research right here on Earth. Scientists study life that lives in extreme environments, like the frozen Arctic and Antarctic, or places with extreme heat, like volcano vents. Organisms that live in such environments are called extremophiles. They might be microbes that can survive in boiling water, steam, high concentrations of salt, methane gas, and even radiation. Studying extremophiles gives scientists a better idea of how life might survive and what it might look like on planets where conditions are also extreme. In Antarctica, the environment in the McMurdo Dry Valleys is similar to the environment on Mars—dry, very cold, and mostly ice-free desert. Bacteria living under rocks in the Antarctic desert could provide clues about how to detect life on Mars or other planets.

Are We Alone?

Since the invention of radio, television, and radar, signals from Earth have wound up getting transmitted into space. A radio wave

HEY, ALIENS, READ THIS!

THE FIRST ATTEMPT TO COMMUNICATE WITH ALIENS occurred in 1974. The Arecibo Observatory in Puerto Rico wanted to demonstrate what its radio telescope—one of the world's largest—could do. It made history by transmitting a three-minute message to M13, the 100,000-star Hercules cluster. The radio message was a series of 1,679 numbers designed to reveal information about mathematics, human DNA, and Earth's location in the solar system. It also included a picture of a human and a telescope. Since M13 is 25,000 light-years away, any reply would take twice that time to return. The Arecibo message was really a symbolic event, though it was still important. It was the first step in thinking about how to best communicate with extraterrestrial beings.

THE ARECIBO MESSAGE, BLASTED INTO SPACE IN 1974, INCLUDED THIS PICTURE.

takes about eight minutes to reach the sun and four years to reach the nearest star. Some scientists think it is possible that other civilizations are transmitting signals, too— we just might not know how to receive them. Another civilization's technology could be more advanced than ours by millions of years.

Rather than just wondering if we are alone in the universe, we can use science and technology to look for intelligent life— beings that use language to communicate. A California institute called SETI, which stands for Search for Extraterrestrial Intelligence, uses its Allen Telescope Array (ATA) to listen for radio signals. It hopes to detect another civilization that uses technology. The organization is also using its scopes to take a closer look at exoplanets in the habitable zone. SETI astrobiologists are trying to discover whether life ever existed on Mars, or whether life might be found in the lakes

THE ALLEN TELESCOPE ARRAY SEARCHES FOR SIGNS OF EXTRATERRESTRIAL INTELLIGENCE.

and oceans on some of Jupiter's and Saturn's moons. Researchers are working on developing a system to search the entire sky for laser flashes that an advanced civilization might use to communicate. With the possibility of at least one planet orbiting every star in the universe, it is reasonable to believe that intelligent life will one day be discovered.

Do You Like This Tune?

In 2017, a group called Messaging Extraterrestrial Intelligence (METI) sent a musical message from Norway to a red dwarf star, GJ 273. Called "Hello," the message will take 12.5 years to arrive and another 12.5 years to receive a reply, if there is one. "Hello" contains radio pulses that click on and off so anyone listening can tell it apart from pulsars and other naturally occurring signals. The message also includes instructions on how to convert the digital signal to sound to listen to its electronic dance music, called techno.

STOP LIGHT POLLUTION

HERE ARE SOME STEPS you and your friends and family can take to limit light pollution.

- Only use as much light as you need. For example, if enough sunlight is coming into your classroom through the windows, leave the light switch off.
- Close blinds and curtains to prevent light from seeping into the outdoors.
- Point light downward at what you need to see, such as a walkway, not up into the sky or other places where it is not needed.
- Encourage the use of shielded lights outside, which stop light from shining upward.
- Avoid outdoor lightbulbs that emit a lot of blue light by choosing products that are described as "warm" and that list a color temperature lower than 3000 kelvins. Look for lights approved by the International Dark-Sky Association.
- Tell other people about the importance of dark skies.

LIGHT POLLUTION AFFECTS THE SKIES ABOVE POPULATED AREAS LIKE CITIES.

Lights Out!

When the sun begins to set, you probably think nothing of switching on the lights and going about your usual activities. Light makes our lives easier, but not all light at night is helpful. Light that causes problems for humans, wildlife, and the environment is called light pollution. Often unnecessary and unwanted, light pollution interferes with natural plant, animal, and human life cycles, because life is adapted to daily periods of light and dark. It also interferes with human activities, including important research—the study of space—and people's ability to see and enjoy the night sky. The stars should be visible to anyone who wants to see them. However, in the United States and Europe, 99 percent of people cannot look up and see a natural dark sky.

Light pollution takes many forms. You might see it as glare when car headlights shine into your eyes, or as over-illumination when more lights than necessary are used. When you see lights shining from an empty skyscraper or office building, you're seeing over-illumination. Another type, called sky glow, is the great hazy dome of light that surrounds towns, cities, and even smaller communities. Light trespass happens when lights spill into areas where no light is needed. Picture a floodlight on a construction site lighting up the surrounding area instead of just the work site. Clutter occurs when too many lights are grouped together, such as collections of billboards and neon lights.

All this light makes it difficult for you to look up at night and see all the sky has to offer. It also makes it hard for astronomers and other scientists to study the night sky. When lights make the night bright, scientists are unable to study dim objects. If astronomers can't observe light in space, they cannot properly explore the universe.

RESEARCH SPACE LIKE ASTRONOMERS MUNAZZA ALAM (RIGHT), HALEY FICA (CENTER), AND SARA CAMNASIO (LEFT)!

Space Jobs

Would you like to go to work ... in *space*? When you think about space jobs, astronaut is probably the first one to come to mind. However, there are many space-industry jobs that do not involve riding a rocket out of the atmosphere. In fact, astronauts could not do their work without all the other specialists in the space program. Many are scientists, but there are plenty of other jobs on the ground, from the people who design and sew space suits to the ground crews who launch rockets.

ENJOY A PLANETARIUM SHOW!

Astronomers study the physical and chemical properties of all matter outside Earth's atmosphere. They design instruments to observe space, and use telescopes for research and computers to analyze their data. Amateur astronomers also study the night sky, but they

THERE ARE PLENTY OF WAYS TO ENJOY SPACE from Earth. You can visit a planetarium—a unique theater with a domed screen that curves overhead like the night sky. A special projector shows stars, planets, and other celestial objects on the screen. Sky shows cover all kinds of topics, from space exploration to constellation identification to the tales ancient cultures told to explain what they saw in the heavens.

Planetariums, as well as observatories and universities, often have large telescopes and events where members of the public can go for a look up. They might host star parties during meteor showers or at other times when interesting objects become visible. Planetariums may be part of science centers, which host exhibits where you can learn about the universe, touch a meteorite or moon rock, or see spacecraft used to explore our solar system. Some science centers, as well as other organizations, offer space camps where kids, teens, and even adults can experience how astronauts train. At space camp, you might launch rockets, work with robots, or tackle engineering challenges. You might even train using a simulator, a machine that lets you feel what it's like to operate a spacecraft.

ON EARTH, ASTRONAUTS AND GEOLOGISTS TEST A LUNAR ROVER AND EQUIPMENT THAT COULD HELP THEM EXPLORE THE MOON'S SURFACE ONE DAY.

A METEOROLOGIST HOLDS A WEATHER BALLOON AT THE NATIONAL WEATHER SERVICE HEADQUARTERS IN STERLING, VIRGINIA, U.S.A.

do it for pleasure, rather than to earn a living. Many amateur astronomers are very knowledgeable, and their observations have aided the work of professional astronomers.

Physicists study the physical properties of matter, energy, space, and time, along with how they interact. Like astronomers, they observe space and develop instruments to better observe the universe. Physicists create theories and laws that explain their observations.

Geologists working in space science study how rocky planets formed. Using satellites, landers, rovers, and other tools, geologists analyze the types of rocks found on planets and other celestial objects.

Meteorologists study Earth's atmosphere and weather, and provide forecasts. They use satellites, as well as ground- and air-based observations to gather information and study the climate— how weather changes over time. The space program depends on meteorologists to determine the best times to launch spacecraft. It also needs accurate predictions to prepare for rocket launches. High winds and lightning can prevent prelaunch preparations and make it impossible to attach a spacecraft to a rocket. Meteorologists also study and track space weather, which can

affect space flight, communication and navigation systems, and electrical power grids.

Astronauts travel beyond Earth's atmosphere to explore space and conduct space research. They have degrees, as well as work experience, in fields that include science, medicine, technology, engineering, and other related areas. Some have piloted jet aircraft. As well as passing a physical exam, astronauts must be able to work as a team and show leadership and communication skills.

Mathematicians use algebra, geometry, and other branches of math to solve problems relating to space science. Their expertise helps design spacecraft, computer software, and other tools needed to explore space.

Chemists study the chemical makeup of objects in space. They use telescopes, space probes, and other tools to analyze objects and look for water and minerals, which could indicate life beyond Earth.

Aerospace engineers design spacecraft and solve problems relating to traveling in the atmosphere and space. Space programs depend on many types of experts, including biomedical, computer, electrical, nuclear, and plastics engineers.

THREE WAYS TO SEE THE NIGHT SKY

WHEN IT COMES TO VIEWING THE NIGHT SKY, you have three choices: NAKED-EYE VIEWING, observing through BINOCULARS, or using a TELESCOPE. The best way to begin is with the naked eye. You can see stars, constellations, meteor showers, satellites, and sometimes a comet with just your eyes. The five closest planets—Mercury, Venus, Mars, Jupiter, and Saturn—can be seen without special equipment, even from cities. You can also observe the moon's phases and lunar eclipses. With safety equipment, you can watch solar eclipses, but remember, it is never safe to look directly at the sun or a solar eclipse. You will find that sometimes the unaided eye is better than binoculars or telescopes, because auroras spread across the sky and constellations are too spread out to see though a lens.

After you've spent some time naked-eye viewing, learn your way around the night sky using binoculars. They show a wider view than a telescope, which makes it easier to find celestial objects. A pair of 8 x 40 binoculars are a good place to start. Large binoculars get too heavy to hold for very long. If your hands shake, the image will be blurry. Binoculars will allow you to see more stars, even if you live where light pollution exists. Look for double stars, star clusters, variable stars, nebulae, and even distant galaxies. A full moon is too bright to look at through binoculars, but it is fun to observe a crescent moon at twilight, when its glare is less intense. Look for craters and the lines radiating from them, called rays, as well as maria, which are plains of hardened lava. Check planet calendars (you can find them with an online search) to find out what planets are visible from your location on specific dates, and look for the planets in our solar system. You can even see four of Jupiter's moons—Ganymede, Io, Europa, and Callisto.

After you are comfortable observing with binoculars, you will be better able to use a telescope. Then you can take a closer look at all the objects you've already found, as well as explore Saturn's rings, distant moons, comets, asteroids, and other deep-sky objects.

A LUNAR ECLIPSE IS VISIBLE WITH THE NAKED EYE.

POINT BINOCULARS AT A WANING MOON FOR THIS VIEW.

USE BINOCULARS TO EXAMINE WHAT YOU CAN SEE WITH THE NAKED EYE IN CLOSER DETAIL.

THE VIEW OF THE MOON AS SEEN THROUGH A TELESCOPE SHOWS LOTS MORE NOOKS AND CRANNIES.

USE A TELESCOPE TO SEE EVEN MORE DETAIL.

SPACE WATCH: SPOT A NAKED-EYE GALAXY!

You can do it! You can spot a galaxy with your feet planted firmly on Earth, and without any special equipment. Here's how to do it.

1. Get ready.

☑ Study a star chart to become familiar with constellations visible from your location.

☑ Plan to use a red light when you look at your sky chart outdoors (see Seeing in the Dark, page 43).

A STAR CHART CAN HELP YOU IDENTIFY CONSTELLATIONS.

2. Choose your time and location.

☑ Find a dark spot without light pollution.

☑ Look at a calendar or moon phase app to see the date of the next new moon. During this period, the moon is not visible. Its location, between Earth and sun, places the moon's lit surface away from Earth. This dark period lasts for just a few days, so choose a clear night close to this date.

3. Look Up

☑ Go outside.

☑ Give your eyes 30 to 40 minutes to get used to the dark.

☑ Look up!

People living in tropical latitudes, south of 20° north, or locations below the Equator can see two irregular galaxies— the **LARGE MAGELLANIC CLOUD** (LMC) and the **SMALL MAGELLANIC CLOUD** (SMC). Hydrus, the Water Snake, will lead you to these neighboring galaxies. Star hop between the stars Beta Hydri and Gamma Hydri to reach the LMC, and follow Beta Hydri toward Alpha Hydri to see the SMC. With the naked eye, both galaxies look like hazy smudges of light in the night sky.

SMALL MAGELLANIC CLOUD

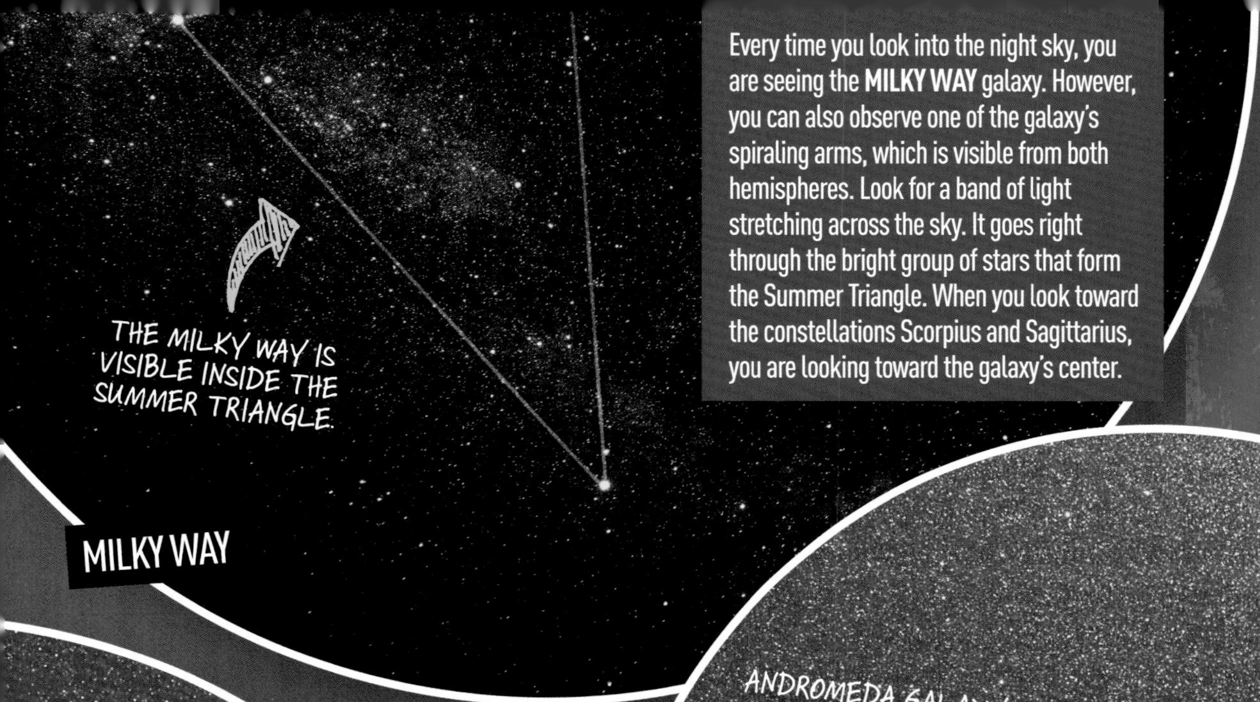

Every time you look into the night sky, you are seeing the **MILKY WAY** galaxy. However, you can also observe one of the galaxy's spiraling arms, which is visible from both hemispheres. Look for a band of light stretching across the sky. It goes right through the bright group of stars that form the Summer Triangle. When you look toward the constellations Scorpius and Sagittarius, you are looking toward the galaxy's center.

THE MILKY WAY IS VISIBLE INSIDE THE SUMMER TRIANGLE.

MILKY WAY

ANDROMEDA GALAXY

MAGELLANIC CLOUDS

ANDROMEDA GALAXY

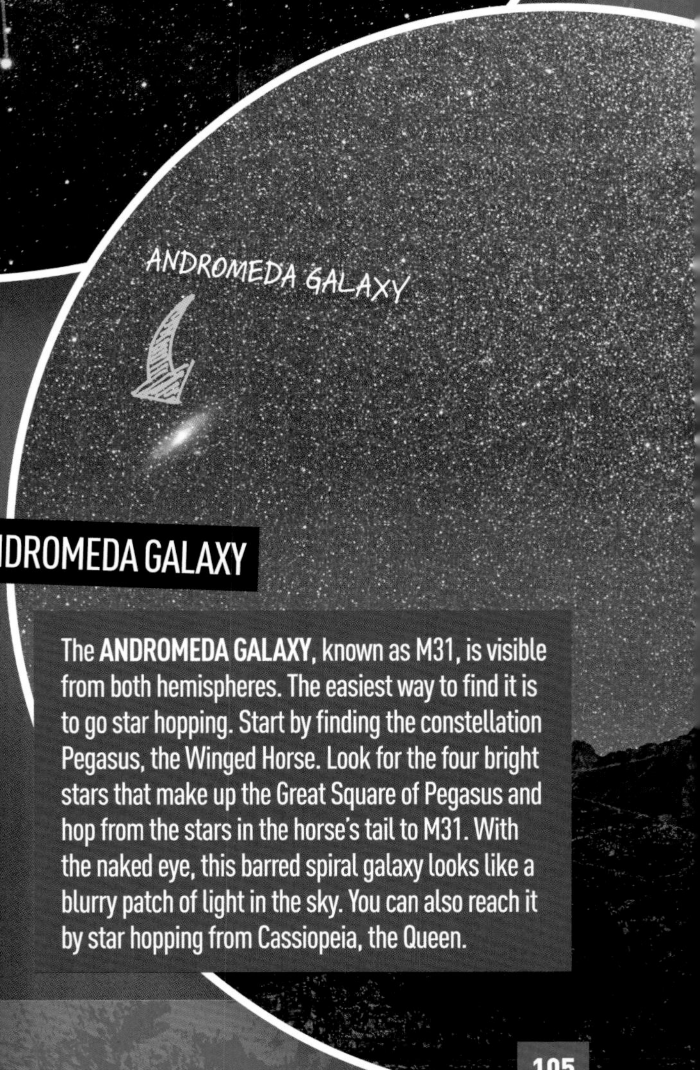

LARGE MAGELLANIC CLOUD

The **ANDROMEDA GALAXY**, known as M31, is visible from both hemispheres. The easiest way to find it is to go star hopping. Start by finding the constellation Pegasus, the Winged Horse. Look for the four bright stars that make up the Great Square of Pegasus and hop from the stars in the horse's tail to M31. With the naked eye, this barred spiral galaxy looks like a blurry patch of light in the sky. You can also reach it by star hopping from Cassiopeia, the Queen.

SPACE LAB

BEND LIGHT—REFLECTION AND REFRACTION IN ACTION

Studying how light behaves on Earth makes it easier to understand how it behaves in space. When light strikes an object, like a mirror, it bounces off it. We call that reflected light. When light travels through a transparent substance, like air or water, it bends. We call that refracted light. Experiment with both in this two-step activity.

STEP ONE: REFLECT LIGHT

What to do:

What you need:

FLASHLIGHT

MIRROR

SPOON

1. **In a windowless room,** turn on the flashlight and set it on a table or other surface, so that the light is visible.

2. **Turn the lights off.**

3. **Hold the mirror in front of the light,** and note what happens to the beam.

4. **Can you direct the light beam at different objects by only turning the mirror?** How does the light look when it strikes different objects?

5. **Get creative.** What happens if you try to reflect the light with the back of a spoon? You could also experiment with a piece of aluminum foil, a quarter, or other shiny surface.

What's Happening

You see direct light from objects that produce their own light, like the sun, a fire, or a lamp. Reflected light, however, allows you to see everything else. When you held the mirror to the flashlight beam, it reflected light in parallel paths. When you reflected light with the convex surface of the spoon, it sent light traveling in more than one direction.

STEP TWO: REFRACT LIGHT

What you need:

PENCIL

A CLEAR DRINKING GLASS, SHORTER THAN YOUR PENCIL

WATER

What to do:

1. Fill the glass three-quarters full with water.

2. Place the pencil in the glass so that it rests against one edge.

3. **Look at the pencil through the side of the glass.** What do you notice?

4. **Now hold the pencil so it stands straight up in the center.** Slowly move it closer to one side, then along the edge of the glass. What is different?

What's Happening

When light travels through a single medium, such as air or water, it travels in a straight line. When passing through two mediums—both water and air—light bends. When the pencil was resting against the edge of the glass, it appeared to bend at the point where the water met the air, because light was refracted as it passed between the boundary of air and water. After passing the boundary, the light traveled in a straight line again, which is why the pencil only looked bent at one spot. When the pencil was upright, it appeared broken, and the part in the water looked wider. This happened as light traveling from the water to the air refracted. The human brain sees this illusion because of the way it processes the refraction of light.

GLOSSARY

asteroid rocky object smaller than a planet, formed in the early stage of our solar system

atmosphere the gases surrounding a space object

axis an imaginary line around which an object rotates

big bang an enormous explosion that scientists believe was the initial event in the formation of the universe

black dwarf the cooling remains of a dwarf star that has used up its nuclear fuel

black hole a place in space with extremely intense gravity from which light cannot escape

brown dwarf a faintly glowing body too small to sustain a nuclear fusion reaction

comet a frozen object made of ice and dust that travels in an elongated orbit around the sun, often causing material to vaporize and form a tail that streams behind it

constellation one of 88 star patterns in the sky recognized by astronomers

corona the outermost layer of gases in the sun's atmosphere

cosmonaut an astronaut in the Russian space program

crater a circular depression in the surface of a planet or moon, caused by a meteorite or asteroid impact or by volcanic action

dark energy the force believed to cause the accelerated expansion of the universe

dark matter an unknown substance that is only detectable by the gravity it exerts

dwarf planet a small object that orbits the sun, has a round shape, and has other objects nearby and within its orbit

eclipse the passing of one space object in front of another, temporarily blocking the distant object's light

frequency the number of waves that pass a point in a certain length of time

fusion the combining of the nuclei of two atoms to form one heavier nucleus, in a process that releases energy

galaxy a collection of stars, gas, and dust, held together by gravity; may contain many billions of stars

gyroscope a device composed of a wheel held in a framework of rings, which allows the wheel to tilt in all directions and spin rapidly; used to sense an object's orientation and keep it level

hemisphere half of a celestial object; on Earth, the Equator divides the Northern and Southern Hemispheres.

International Astronomical Union an organization of international members who work together to promote, develop, and safeguard the science of astronomy

kelvin a temperature scale that has the same increments as the Celsius scale but begins at a point known as absolute zero (-273.15°C; -459.67°F)

Kuiper belt a doughnut-shaped region that begins just beyond the orbit of Neptune, containing many icy objects in orbit around the sun

light pollution unwanted artificial light, such as the haze or glare that washes out views of the night sky

light-year the distance light can travel in one year, equaling 5.88 trillion miles (9.46 trillion km)

luminosity the inherent brightness of an object in space, which differs from its apparent brightness which decreases with distance

magnitude a number measuring an astronomical body's brightness

main sequence star a star, in the longest stage of its cycle, fusing hydrogen into helium in its core

mass the total quantity of material in an object

meteor an object from space that appears as a streak of light when it passes through Earth's atmosphere

meteorite a meteor that has landed on Earth

meteoroid a rocky object in space, smaller than an asteroid

microgravity gravity so weak that objects seem weightless

NASA an acronym for the U.S. government space agency, the National Aeronautics and Space Administration

nebula a glowing cloud of gas and dust in space

neutron star a small, very compact star of tightly packed neutrons, formed from a supernova

Oort cloud an enormous region of space around the solar system, containing mainly icy objects such as comets

orbit the path a celestial object follows as it revolves around another body

planet a large round object that orbits a star in a path free of space debris

planetary nebula the glowing cloud of gas resulting from a supernova

plasma an electrically charged gas

pulsar a rapidly spinning neutron star that emits regular pulses of radio waves

quasar a very bright, rare object in space that produces strong radio waves

red dwarf a faint star, about half the size of the sun

red giant an aging, low-mass star greatly expanded from its original size, with a cooler temperature than other stars

ring a band of material around a planet, formed of particles ranging in size from dust to boulders

satellite an object orbiting another object, which may be naturally occurring or human-made

solar mass a unit equaling the mass of the sun, which is used to compare the masses of stars and other celestial objects

solar wind a stream of high-energy particles flowing from the sun or another star

spiral galaxy a galaxy with a pinwheel shape

star a hot, giant, glowing ball of gas held together by its own gravity

supergiant a very massive, bright star with a short life span

supernova the violent, luminous explosion at the end of a massive star's life

wavelength the distance between two identical points on two waves next to each other

white dwarf the very hot, white, final phase of some stars, such as the sun

INDEX

Boldface indicates illustrations.

A
Active galaxies, 60–61, 63
Air resistance, 14, **14**
Alam, Munazza, **6,** 7, 10, 48–49, **49,** 70, **71,** 94, **94, 101**
Aldrin, Buzz, **74,** 84
Allen Telescope Array (ATA), 99, **99**
Andromeda galaxy, 14, 96, 105, **105**
Antarctica, 97–98
Armstrong, Neil, 84
Arnold, Ricky, **85**
Asteroid belt, **24,** 38, **38**
Asteroids, 13, 18–19, 38, **38,** 40
Astronauts
    becoming, 87, 101
    radiation dangers to, 98
    and space exploration, 74, **74**
    space suits for, 85–86
Astronomical unit, 27
Astronomy, 7, 10–11, 48, 55, 85, 100–102
Atmosphere
    and beginning of space, 12–13, **12**
    of exoplanets, 7, 70, 94
    and life on Earth, 27
    of planets, 24–35, 70
Auroras, **8–9,** 13, **13,** 41, **41**

B
Big bang, 23, 96, **96**
Binary star systems, 54, **54,** 57–58, **58,** 74
Binoculars, 103, **103**
Biosignatures, 94–95
Black holes, 13, 54–55, **54, 55,** 61–62, 64, 66–67, **66–67**
Burbank, Dan, **86**

C
Camnasio, Sara, **71, 101**
Cassini-Huygens spacecraft, 76–77, **76**
Cepheids, 57, **57**
Ceres, 18, 37
Clusters, 16, 19, **19,** 96, **96**
Comets, 13, 17, 18–19, 39, 40, **40,** 77–78, **78**
Communication with extraterrestrial life, 98–99
Compound telescopes, 72
Coronal mass ejections (CMEs), 21
Cryovolcanoes, 35

D
Dark energy, 13, 97
Dark matter, 13, 97, **97**
Dark skies, 100
Deep Impact mission, 77
Dwarf planets, 18, 25, 36–37, **36–37**
Dwarf stars, 21–22, **51,** 52–53, **52,** 54

E
Earth
    composition of, 27–28, **27**
    gravity of, 15
    life on, 27, 94
    magnetic field of, 39
    orbital velocity of, **17**
    as terrestrial planet, 18, 24
    water on, 18, **18,** 22, 27, 41, 94
Elements, 23

Employment in space-related fields, 101–2, **101, 102**
Eris, 35, 37, **37**
Exoplanets, 7, 58–59, **59,** 70, 94
Exosphere, **12**
Explorer 1, 39
Explorer 3, 39
Extraterrestrial life, 94–95, **95,** 98–99
Extravehicular Mobility Unit (EMU), 85–86
Extremely Large Telescopes (ELTs), 94
Extremophiles, 98

F
Fica, Haley, **71, 101**
Flyby spacecraft, 75

G
Galactic address, 18–19, **18–19**
Galactic cosmic rays (GCRs), 98
Galaxies
    active galaxies, 60–61, 63
    barred spiral galaxy NGC 1672, **92–93**
    clusters of, 16, 19, **19,** 96, **96**
    measuring distances to, 57
    naked-eye viewing of, 104–5, **104–5**
    radio galaxies, 60–61, **61, 63**
    Seyfert galaxies, 60, **60**
    see also Milky Way
Galilei, Galileo, **24,** 25, 30
Gas giant planets, 24
Giant stars, 22, **22,** 51–52, **51**
Global Positioning System (GPS), 79
Goldilocks zone, 94, 98
Gravity
    and dark matter, 97
    and distance, 14
    experiments with, 44–45, **44–45**
    and formation of solar system, 18–19
    and ISS, 86
    and laws of motion, 16, 80
    on Mars, 28
    and mass, 14–15, **15**
    on Mercury, 26
    spacecraft escaping, 75
    and stars, 50, 52–55
    on Uranus, 33
    on Venus, 33
Great Red Spot, 29, **30–31**

H
Halley's Comet, **11,** 35, 40
Haumea, 18, 35, **36,** 37
Helium, 20, 21–22, 23, **23**
Herschel, William, 32
Hot Jupiters, 6, 58–59, 70
Hubble, Edwin, 75
Hubble Space Telescope, 7, **7,** 75, **75,** 80, 89, **89, 91**
Hydrogen, 19, 20–23, 24, 29–30, 32–34, 50–53

I
Inertia, 16
International Space Station (ISS), **2–3,** 13, 45, **45,** 72, 80, 81, **81,** 83–86, **85, 86,** 89, **89**
ISS. *see* International Space Station (ISS)

J
James Webb Space Telescope, 94, **95**
Joint Polar Satellite System, 80

Juno spacecraft, **1**
Jupiter
    atmosphere of, 24
    general facts about, 29–30, **29, 30–31**
    gravity of, 15
    moons of, 25, 30, **30**
    orbital velocity of, **17**
    spacecraft missions to, 1

K
Kármán Line, 12–13, **12**
Kepler Space Telescope, 59, **59**
Kitt Peak National Observatory, 10, **11**
Kuiper, George, 35
Kuiper belt, 18, 25, 35
Kuiper belt objects (KBO), 35, **35,** 36, 37

L
Laniakea group of galaxies, **18–19,** 19
Life
    on Earth, 27, 94
    on other planets, 94–95, **95,** 98–99
Light
    reflection and refraction of, 72, 106–7, **106–7**
    wavelengths of, 7
Light pollution, 100, **100**
Light-year, 14
Local Group, 19, 96, **96**

M
Magellan 1 Baade telescope, **49, 71**
Magellanic Clouds, **49, 104–5**
Magnetic fields, 20, 25, 26, 27, 39, 41, 61, 63, 98
Magnetosphere, 39, **98**
Magnitude, 56
Main sequence stars, 21, 50–51, **51,** 52
Makemake, 18, 35, 37
Mars
    general facts about, 28
    gravity of, 15
    moons of, 28, **29**
    orbital velocity of, **17**
    temperature of, 94
    as terrestrial planet, 18
Mars Pathfinder rovers, **28,** 73, 77, **77**
Mass
    and gravity, 14–15, **15**
    and stars, 51–53, 63, 64
Mercury, **17,** 18, 24–26, **26,** 32, 51, 74, 103
Mesosphere, **12**
Messaging Extraterrestrial Intelligence (METI), 99
Metalloids, 23
Metals, 23, **23**
Meteoroids, 41–43, **41–43**
Meteors, 12, 13, 41–43
Meteor showers, 41, **41–43,** 42–43
Milky Way
    black hole of, 61
    galactic address of, **18–19,** 19
    and Local Group, 19, 96, **96**
    naked-eye viewing of, **105**
    number of stars in, 16
    as type of galaxy, 60
    viewing from Earth, 10, 12, **12**
Mir space station, **82**
Moon (Earth), 15, 24–25, **25,** 27–28, 103, **103**
Moons
    of Eris, 37
    of Jupiter, 25, 30, **30**
    of Mars, 28, **29**
    naming of, 34, **34**
    as satellites, 17
    of Saturn, 25, **30,** 31–32, **32,** 76–77
    of Uranus, 34
Motion, laws of, 16

N

Naked-eye viewing, 103–5, **103, 105**
NASA (National Aeronautics and Space Administration)
  and Cassini-Huygens mission, 77
  and Deep Impact mission, 77
  Extravehicular Mobility Unit, 85
  and Kepler Space Telescope, 59
  Mars rover missions, 73, 77
  planned Mars mission by, 28
  sky-viewing app from, 88–89
  and space race, 84
  and space shuttles, 80
  as U.S. space agency, 83
Nebulae, 50
Neptune, **17,** 18, 34–35, **34, 35**
Neutrinos, 97
Neutron stars, **52,** 53, 63, **63**
Newton, Isaac, 16, 44, **44**
Night vision, 43
Nitrogen, 12
Nonmetals, 23
Nuclear fusion, 18–19, 20

O

Observatories, 10–11, **11,** 97, **97**
Observatory spacecraft, 78, **78**
Oort, Jan, 39
Oort cloud, 19, 25, 39, **39**
Orbital sunrise, **13**
Orbits
  of asteroids, 38
  of comets, 40
  and gravity, 15
  of Jupiter's moons, 30
  and laws of motion, 16
  shapes of, 17
Oxygen, 12

P

Parkes Radio Telescope, 73, **73**
Penetrator spacecraft, 77–78, **78**
Photons, 10
Planetariums, 101, **101**
Planetary nebulae, 52, **52**
Planet Nine, 36, **36**
Planets
  definition of, **25**
  orbital velocity of, **17**
  of solar system, 18–19, 24, **24,** 25–35
  viewing in night sky, 103
  see also specific planets
Pluto, 18, 25, **25,** 35, 36–37, **36**
Pope, Alexander, 34
Protostars, 50, **50**
Pulsars, 13, 62, **62**

Q

Quasars, 13, 60, **60,** 63, **63,** 74

R

Radiation, 61, 73, 98
Radio galaxies, 60–61, **61,** 63
Radio lobes, 63, **63**
Radio telescopes, **11,** 60, **61,** 73–74, **73, 74,** 98–99
Reflector telescopes, 72
Refractor telescopes, 72
Research, 70–71
Rings
  of Saturn, 31, **31**
  of Uranus, **33**
Rockets, 75, 80–81, **80,** 90–91, **90–91**

S

Satellites, 17, 75, 79–80, **79,** 88, **88**
Saturn
  Cassini-Huygens mission to, 76–77

general facts about, 31–32, **31**
moons of, 25, **30,** 32, **32,** 76–77
orbital velocity of, **17**
Search for Extraterrestrial Intelligence (SETI), 99
Seyfert galaxies, 60, **60**
Shakespeare, William, 34
Shepard, Alan, 84
Shkaplerov, Anton, **86**
Skylab, **82**
Sky-watching, 88–89, 103, **103,** 104–5
Solar flares, 21, **98**
Solar nebulae, 18
Solar particle radiation, 98
Solar system, formation of, 18–19, **24,** 40
Solar wind, 39
South Pole Neutrino Observatory, 97, **97**
Space
  beginning of, 12–13
  distances in, 13–14
  existence of life in, 94–95, **95,** 98–99
  galactic address of Earth, 18–19, **18–19**
  and gravity, 14–15
  motion in, 16
Space agencies, 81, 83
Space camps, 101
Spacecraft
  artificial satellites, 17, 75, 79–80, **79,** 88, **88**
  flyby missions with, 75
  landers, 77
  multiple-vehicle missions, 76–77
  orbital missions, 76
  penetrators, 77–78, **78**
  rovers, **28,** 73, 74, 77, **77**
  spacecraft buses, **78,** 79
  see also specific spacecraft
Space exploration
  Earth-based, 72–74
  with robotic vehicles, 74
  with spacecraft, 74–81, 83, 84
  space stations, **82**
  space walks, 68–69, 85
  see also Spacecraft
Space jobs, 101–2, **101, 102**
Space Lab experiments
  black holes, 66–67
  gravity, 44–45
  light-bending, 106–7
  rockets, 90–91
Space litter, 83, **83,** 88
Space Race, 84, **84**
Space shuttles, 75, 80, **80, 81, 89**
Space suits, 85–86
Space walks, 68–69
Spitzer space telescope, 78–79, **78**
Sputnik 1, 75, 84, **84**
Star-finding charts, 104, **104**
Stars
  binary star systems, 54, **54,** 57–58, **58,** 74
  black holes, **53,** 54–55, **54, 55,** 61–62, 64, 66–67
  collapse of, 53–54, **53**
  dwarf stars, 21–22, **51,** 52–53, **52,** 54
  finding in the night sky, **64–65**
  formation of, 50, **50**
  giant stars, 22, **22,** 51–52, **51**
  main sequence stars, 21, 50–51, **51,** 52
  number in Milky Way, 12, 16
  variable stars, 55, 56, **56,** 57, **57**
  see also Astronomy
Stellar jets, **46–47**
Stratosphere, **12**
Summer Triangle, **105**
Sun
  composition of, 20–21
  formation of, 19

gravity of, 15
image from extreme ultraviolet imaging telescope, 20
layers of, **22**
life cycle of, 21–22
light of, 13
size of, **20–21,** 21
statistics on, **21**
Sunspots, 20–21
Superclusters, 19
Supernovae, 53–54, **53,** 57, **63,** 66

T

Technology spin-offs, 85
Telescopes, 10–11, **11,** 48, **48, 49,** 60, **70, 71,** 72–75, **72, 73, 74,** 78, **78,** 94, 103
Terrestrial planets, 18, 24
Thermosphere, **12**
Tiangong-1 space station, **82**
Tides, 15
Troposphere, **12**

U

U.S. National Oceanic and Atmospheric Administration (NOAA), 80
Universe
  beginning of, 96, **96**
  dark matter and energy in, 13, 97, **97**
  extraterrestrial life in, 94–95, **95,** 98–99
  size of, 19
Uranus, **17,** 32–34, **33,** 36

V

Van Allen, James, 39
Van Allen belts, 39, **39,** 98
Van Kármán, Theodore, 12
Variable stars, 55, 56, **56,** 57, **57**
Venus, **17,** 18, 24, 26–27, **26,** 33, 51, 70, 94, 103
Very Large Array (VLA), 74, **74**
Very Long Baseline Array (VLBA), 74
Virgo supercluster, **18–19,** 19
Voyager 1, 30
Voyager 2, 75

W

Water
  and comets, 40, 78
  on Earth, 18, **18,** 22, 27, 41, 94
  on exoplanets, 94
  and hydrogen, 23
  on ISS, 85
  and life, 27, 98
  on Neptune, 34–35
  and refraction of light, 106–7
  on Saturn's moons, 32
  on Uranus's moons, 34

CREDITS

ASP: Alamy; GI: Getty Images; NGC: National Geographic Image Collection; SCI: Science Source; SS: Shutterstock

1, NASA/Bill Ingalls; 2-3, NASA/Goddard Space Flight Center; 4 (rocket), Den Rozhnovsky/SS; 4 (Mars), Nerthuz/SS; 4 (moon), Pe3k/SS; 4 (Earth), Rashevskyi Viacheslav/SS; 4 (LE), Denis Belitsky/SS; 4 (RT), NASA, ESA, and the Hubble SM4 ERO Team; 4 (rocket), mimka/SS; 5 (UP LE), aapsky/SS; 5 (LE), NASA; 5 (RT), NASA/ESA; 5 (LO RT), ALEX S/SS; 6, Becky Hale/NG Studio; 7, NASA; 8-9, Denis Belitsky/SS; 10 (UP), Randall Scott/NGC; 10 (LO), Maiara Martins/SS; 11 (UP LE), Frank Zullo/SCI; 11 (UP RT), ALEX S/SS; 11 (LO), Susan E. Degginger/ASP; 12 (LE), Kevin Key/SS; 12 (RT), Andramin/SS; 13 (UP), WanRu Chen/GI; 13 (LO), NASA; 14 (UP), ESA/Hubble & NASA; 14 (LO), maxpro/SS; 15 (books), Micah Schmidt; 15 (melon), Maks Narodenko/SS; 15 (elephant), gualtiero boffi/SS; 15 (moon), Pe3k/SS; 15 (Mars), Nerthuz/SS; 15 (Earth), Rashevskyi Viacheslav/SS; 15 (Jupiter), Nerthuz/SS; 16, Carl Schneider/GI; 17, Mark Garlick/SCI; 18, steinliland/GI; 18-19, muratart/SS; 19, NASA/Goddard Space Flight Center/Scientific Visualization Studio/ESA/L. Bradley/JHU; 20, ESA/NASA/SOHO; 20-21, Yuliia Markova/SS; 22 (UP), Siberian Art/SS; 22 (LO), CahekZ/SS; 23 (UP), TinnaPong/SS; 23 (LO), William Bunce/ASP; 24 (UP), Mopic/SS; 24 (LO), iryna1/SS; 25 (UP), Science Photo Library/ASP; 25 (LO), NASA/Johns Hopkins University Applied Physics Laboratory/Southwest Research Institute; 26 (UP), NASA/Johns Hopkins University Applied Physics Laboratory/Carnegie Institution of Washington; 26 (LO), NASA/JPL; 27 (UP), Darren Tierney/SS; 27 (LO), Gary Hincks/SCI; 28, NASA/JPL; 29 (Phobos), NASA/JPL-Caltech/University of Arizona; 29 (Deimos), NASA/JPL-Caltech/University of Arizona; 29 (LO), NASA/JPL/University of Arizona; 30 (UP), NASA/JPL/University of Arizona; 30 (LO), NASA/JPL; 30-31, NASA/JPL-Caltech/SwRI/MSSS/Gerald Eichstadt/Sean Doran; 31 (CTR), NASA/JPL/Space Science Institute; 31 (LO), NASA/JPL/Space Science Institute; 32 (UP LE), ESA/NASA/JPL/University of Arizona; 32 (UP RT), NASA/JPL/Space Science Institute; 32 (LO), NASA/JPL-Caltech/Space Science Institute; 33 (UP), NASA/JPL; 33 (LO), Lawrence Sromovsky, University of Wisconsin-Madison/W.W. Keck Observatory; 34 (UP), eurobanks/SS; 34 (LO), NASA/JPL; 35 (LE), NASA/JPL; 35 (RT), Lynette Cook/SCI; 36 (LE), Caltech/R. Hurt (IPAC); 36-37 (CTR), NASA/APL/SwRI; 36-37 (LO), Diego Barucco/SS; 37 (UP), IMG Stock Studio/SS; 37 (LO), ESO/L. Calçada and Nick Risinger (skysurvey.org); 38, Roger Harris/SCI; 39 (UP), Spencer Sutton/SCI; 39 (LO), NASA/Van Allen Probes/Goddard Space Flight Center; 40 (UP), Photographer/SS; 40 (LO), Frank Zullo/SCI; 41 (UP), Alan Dyer/VWPics/ASP; 41 (LO), Rowan Romeyn/ASP; 42 (UP), vectorlight/SS; 42 (LO LE), Belish/SS ; 42 (LO RT), Wisanu Boonrawd/ASP; 43, Brittny/SS; 44 (Newton), Science History Images/ASP; 44 (pen), Designs Stock/SS; 44 (cup), Feng Yu/SS; 44 (sink), Ari N/SS; 44 (stool), Tatiana Popova/SS; 45 (UP), Micah Schmidt; 45 (LO), NASA; 46-47, NASA, ESA, and the Hubble SM4 ERO Team; 48 (UP), Randall Scott/NGC; 48 (LO), Maiara Martins/SS; 49 (UP LE), Jacqueline Faherty/NGC; 49 (UP RT), ALEX S/SS; 49 (LO), Ryan Trainor; 50, NASA/JPL-Caltech/ESA, the Hubble Heritage Team (STScI/AURA) and IPHAS; 51 (UP), Designua/SS; 51 (LO), ALMA (ESO/NAOJ/NRAO)/E. O'Gorman/P. Kervella; 52 (UP), NASA/GSFC; 52 (LO), NASA and The Hubble Heritage Team (STScI/AURA); 52-53, NASA, ESA, and G. Bacon (STScI); 53 (UP), NASA/DOE/Fermi LAT Collaboration, CXC/SAO/JPL-Caltech/Steward/O. Krause et al., and NRAO/AUI; 53 (LO), ESA/Hubble & NASA; 54 (UP), David Ducros/SCI; 54 (CTR), EHT Collaboration; 54 (LO), NASA/JPL-Caltech; 55, NASA/JPL-Caltech; 56 (UP), angelinast/SS; 56 (CTR), Aaron McCoy/GI; 56 (LO), welcomia/SS ; 57 (LE), NASA/ESA/Hubble Heritage (STScI/AURA)-Hubble/Europe Collab; 57 (RT), Hubble Legacy Archive, NASA, ESA, 58 (UP), Jazziel/SS; 58 (RT), DAVIDE DE MARTIN/SCI; 59 (UP), NASA/JPL-Caltech; 59 (LO), NASA/Troy Cryder; 60 (UP), ESO/R. Gendler; 60 (LO), ESO/M. Kornmesser; 61 (UP), ESO; 61 (LO), Manamana/SS; 62, Jurik Peter/SS; 63 (UP), NASA/JPL-Caltech; 63 (LO LE), NASA, ESA, S. Baum and C. O'Dea (RIT), R. Perley and W. Cotton (NRAO/AUI/NSF), and the Hubble Heritage Team (STScI/AURA); 63 (LO RT), ESA/Hubble, NASA, Suyu et al.; 65, mimka/SS; 64-65, shooarts/SS; 66 (UP LE), marre/SS; 66 (baseball), Maks Narodenko/SS; 66 (marbles), zairiazmal/SS; 66 (girls), Kite_rin/SS; 66 (shirt), Khvost/SS; 67 (UP), Micah Schmidt; 67 (LO), Micah Schmidt; 67 (LO RT), marre/SS; 68-69, NASA; 70 (UP), Randall Scott/NGC; 70 (LO), Maiara Martins/SS; 71 (UP LE), Becky Hale/NG Studio; 71 (UP RT), ALEX S/SS; 71 (LO), Jacqueline Faherty/NGC; 72 (LO), Sharon Rose/ASP; 73 (UP), FooTToo/SS; 73 (LO), Bill Bachman/ASP; 74 (UP), NASA (see individual web page for full credit); 74 (LO LE), Phil Degginger/ASP; 74 (LO RT), Science Photo Library/ASP; 75, NASA; 76 (UP), NASA/JPL-Caltech; 76 (LO), ESA/D. DUCROS; 77, NASA/JPL; 78 (UP), NASA/JPL-Caltech/UMD; 78 (CTR), NASA/JPL-Caltech; 78 (LO), NASA; 79, NASA Earth Observatory; 80 (UP), NASA/Jack Pfaller; 80 (LO), NASA/Carla Cioffi; 81 (CTR), NASA; 81 (LO), NASA; 82 (UP), NASA; 82 (CTR), NASA; 82 (LO), Alejo Miranda/SS; 83, NASA/GSFC/JSC; 84 (UP), NASA; 84 (LO), Sovfoto/Universal Images Group via GI; 85, NASA; 86, NASA; 87 (team), Rawpixel.com/SS; 87 (pilot), PeopleImages/GI; 87 (notecards), Eiko Tsuchiya/SS; 87 (girl), Africa Studio/SS; 87 (class), Monkey Business Images/SS; 87 (scientist), Have a nice day Photo/SS; 87 (swimmer), Suzanne Tucker/SS; 87 (astronaut), ALEX S/SS; 88 (UP), aapsky/SS; 88 (LE), QuickStartProjects/SS; 88 (RT), Alistair Scott/ASP; 89 (UP), NASA; 89 (LO), NASA; 90 (UP), Den Rozhnovsky/SS; 90 (CTR), LightField Studios/SS ; 90 (LO), Micah Schmidt; 91 (straw), AlexandrBognat/SS; 91 (scissors), Kozak Sergii/SS; 91 (tape), Carolyn Franks/SS; 91 (pencil), Vitaly Zorkin/SS; 92-93, NASA/ESA; 94 (UP), Randall Scott/NGC; 94 (LO), Maiara Martins/SS; 95 (UP LE), ESA; 95 (UP RT), ALEX S/SS; 95 (LO), NASA/Ames/SETI Institute/JPL-Caltech; 96 (LE), Stocktrek Images/NGImage Collection; 96 (RT), David Parker/SCI; 97 (UP), Xinhua/ASP; 97 (LO), NASA, ESA, CFHT, CXO, M.J. Jee (University of California, Davis), and A. Mahdavi (San Francisco State University); 98, NASA/MSFC; 99 (UP), SPL/SCI; 99 (LO), Mark Thiessen/NGC; 100, Martin Podzorny/SS; 101 (UP), Jacqueline Faherty/NGC; 101 (LO), Hero Images/GI; 102 (LE), NASA; 102 (RT), Benjamin C. Tankersley/For The Washington Post via GI; 102 (RT), Benjamin C. Tankersley/For The Washington Post via GI; 103 (UP), Grzegorz Lukacijewski/SS ; 103 (CTR), Manisa Pattanayak/Stockimo/ASP; 103 (CTR LE), Roland Magnusson/SS; 103 (LO), Nikita Siyalov/SS; 103 (LO LE), mimka/SS; 104, wonderlandstock/ASP; 104-105, Luis Argerich/SCI; 105 (UP), sripfoto/SS ; 105 (LO), MarcelClemens/SS; 106 (UP LE), Macrovector/SS; 106 (mirror), Stephen Chai/SS; 106 (spoon), onair/SS; 106 (flashlight), Brittny/SS; 107, SPL/SCI

To Amma & Baba, you are my everything. —MA

For Grant, who shares my interest in everything space. —JMG

Since 1888, the National Geographic Society has funded more than 12,000 research, exploration, and preservation projects around the world. The Society receives funds from National Geographic Partners, LLC, funded in part by your purchase. A portion of the proceeds from this book supports this vital work. To learn more, visit natgeo.com/info.

NATIONAL GEOGRAPHIC and Yellow Border Design are trademarks of the National Geographic Society, used under license.

For more information, visit nationalgeographic.com, call 1-877-873-6846, or write to the following address:

National Geographic Partners
1145 17th Street N.W.
Washington, D.C. 20036-4688 U.S.A.

Visit us online at nationalgeographic.com/books

For librarians and teachers: nationalgeographic.com/books /librarians-and-educators

More for kids from National Geographic: natgeokids.com

National Geographic Kids magazine inspires children to explore their world with fun yet educational articles on animals, science, nature, and more. Using fresh storytelling and amazing photography, Nat Geo Kids shows kids ages 6 to 14 the fascinating truth about the world—and why they should care.
kids.nationalgeographic.com/subscribe

For rights or permissions inquiries, please contact National Geographic Books Subsidiary Rights: bookrights@natgeo.com

Produced by Girl Friday Productions

National Geographic supports K–12 educators with ELA Common Core Resources. Visit natgeoed.org/commoncore for more information.

Acknowledgments
I would like to recognize the kind assistance given by Douglas Hube, professor emeritus of physics at the University of Alberta and former national president (1994–96) of the Royal Astronomical Society of Canada, Ian R. Mann, professor of physics at the University of Alberta, and James Kaler, professor emeritus of astronomy at the University of Illinois, for generosity in sharing their vast astronomy expertise. My sincere gratitude extends to Grant Wiens for cheerfully taking care of so many of life's day-to-day details as I focused on this most engaging project. Thanks also to Leah Jenness and the other professionals at Girl Friday Productions, as well as National Geographic Kids, for the genuine pleasure of working together. —JMG

Library of Congress Cataloging-in-Publication Data
Names: Galat, Joan Marie, 1963- author.
Title: Space / by Joan Marie Galat.
Other titles: Absolute expert.
Description: Washington : National Geographic Kids, [2020] | Series: Absolute expert | Includes index. | Audience: 008-012 | Audience: 4-6 | Summary: "Ready to go on an out-of-this world adventure? Travel across the Milky Way and into new galaxies to explore every corner of space so YOU can become an absolute expert. Get up close to the sun and moon, asteroids and comets. Learn about the Oort cloud, supernovae, black holes, and rockets and other spacecraft. Discover the incredible work of astronauts, astronomers, physicists, and other cool space scientists. On this journey across the universe, you'll make your way from our familiar home here on Earth to planets and solar systems that are many light-years away. Rub elbows with the stars on this cosmic adventure complete with special features, sidebars, wacky trivia, and more."-- Provided by publisher.
Identifiers: LCCN 2019034674 | ISBN 9781426336690 (hardcover) | ISBN 9781426336706 (library binding)
Subjects: LCSH: Astronomy--Juvenile literature. | Outer space--Exploration--Juvenile literature.
Classification: LCC QB46 .G273 2020 | DDC 523--dc23
LC record available at https://lccn.loc.gov/2019034674

Printed in China
20/RRDH/1

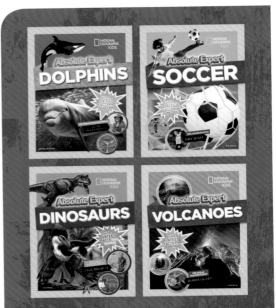

There are more amazing Absolute Expert subjects to explore!

Go to **natgeokids.com**